Heinemann Educational Publishers
Halley Court, Jordan Hill, Oxford OX2 8EJ
A division of Reed Educational and Professional Publishing Ltd

OXFORD MADRID ATHENS FLORENCE
PRAGUE CHICAGO PORTSMOUTH NH (USA)
MEXICO CITY SÃO PAULO SINGAPORE
KUALA LUMPUR TOKYO MELBOURNE
AUCKLAND NAIROBI KAMPALA
IBADAN GABORONE JOHANNESBURG

First published 1997

2001 2000 99 98 97
10 9 8 7 6 5 4 3 2 1

ISBN 0 435 10254 0

Designed and typeset by Jim Turner, The Ascenders Partnership
Cover design by Miller, Craig and Cocking
Illustrations by Pantelis Palios
Printed and bound in the UK by Bath Press

Acknowledgements
The Authors and Publishers should like to thank the following for permission to use copyright material:
Extract from *Merry Christmas Mr Larry* by Larry Hollingworth on p37: William Heinemann; extract from *A time to dance, no time to weep* by Rumer Godden on p41: Macmillan General Books; extract 'Anaheim: Disneyland and Around' on p56: from *The Rough Guide to the USA* by Sam Cook, Jamie Jensen, Tim Perry and Greg Ward (3rd edition, 1996, Rough Guides, London); article 'Dinner Hatched' on p75: *Daily Mail*, 14/11/1996; article 'Hermie the hamster demolished our pub' on p84: *Just Seventeen*, 25/2/1997; article 'Fashion victims' on p85: *Daily Express*, 30/8/96; article 'The Model Railway Passenger' by Jonathan Prynn, from *The Times*, 21/8/1996 on p86: © Times Newspapers Ltd, 1996.

The Publishers have made every effort to trace the copyright holders, but if they have inadvertently overlooked any, they will be pleased to make the necessary arrangements at the first opportunity.

Introduction

Get it Right! is designed to help you prepare for your written examination in English. Like many students, you may wonder how or whether you can revise for your English examination: writing is a skill you have been practising all the way through school, so what can you do to improve your writing in the year before the exam? There is no content to *learn* for an English examination, so how can you revise? However, writing in timed conditions can be a nerve-wracking experience so you may feel you should be doing *something* to prepare for it.

The good news is that there *are* ways in which you can prepare for your English exam. To ensure that you give yourself the best possible chance of gaining the highest grade you can make sure that:

- You understand what an examiner is looking for when she or he marks your written work - Chapter 1 will help you to do this.
- You are ready to organise your writing in the examination - Chapter 2 will help you to do this.
- Your writing, grammar, spelling and punctuation skills are all up to scratch - Chapters 3, 4 and 5 will help you to do this. Chapter 6 lists the common errors students make when writing in timed conditions. Reading and working through this chapter will help you to avoid these pitfalls.

You can use this book in various ways:

- You can work through the book from beginning to end to make sure you practise all key areas. You will find it particularly useful to work through Chapters 1 and 2.
- You can diagnose your own writing using the model in Chapter 1 (page 7) to see which areas you most need to practise.
- Your teacher or tutor may highlight particular areas in your own writing which you should practise.

Do remember that however good your answers are to the **Self-test** and **Writing practice** sections, what counts is how far you use these skills in *your own writing*. Get into the habit of planning your writing carefully and checking it for accuracy as you write. It becomes easier once you understand what to look for!

Contents

pages

1 Meet the examiner 6–14

A short introduction which draws your attention to some of the key points you need to think about when preparing for the exam.

2 Organising your writing 15–30

How to analyse the writing task you are set, especially in terms of audience and purpose. How to plan, research and write a good exam answer.

3 Sentences and paragraphs 31–58

A simple introduction to how sentences are constructed. Even if you don't know any grammar at all, this chapter explains all the ideas and technical terms you need to understand simple grammar. It goes through the commonest mistakes people make when writing sentences and explains how to avoid them. At the end, there is a section about how to use paragraphs correctly.

4 Punctuation 59–87

All the rules of punctuation are explained in this chapter with plenty of practice exercises.

5 Words and spelling 88–113

Advice on how to develop and use your vocabulary effectively. How words are constructed and how to use a knowledge of stems, prefixes and suffixes to build your vocabulary. Advice on how to improve your spelling, followed by the main spelling rules and organised lists of words that cause problems.

6 Common errors 114–127

An alphabetical list of mistakes and confusions that students often make, with an explanation of what is wrong and what is correct.

7 Reference 128–138

An alphabetical list of the technical terms you may come across when people are talking about writing and the English language. Each term is explained in simple English. The list includes all the terms used in this book with references to the pages where the topics are covered in more detail. It also includes a number of other technical terms that you may come across, again with explanations.

8 Answers to self-tests 139–160

Not all the self-tests have answers (some of them are about analysing your own writing). But for those that do, the answers are printed in this chapter, together with explanations.

1 Meet the examiner

One of the problems about doing exams is that you do not know who is going to read what you write, or what they will do with it. The following pages give you a chance to think about what the people who mark your work are looking for.

Your chance to be an examiner

On pages 8 and 9 there are two pieces of descriptive writing. Both were written as answers to the same question:

> *A local newspaper is running a series called 'Snapshot' in which local places of interest are described. Write an entry for the series.*

Before you read the answers, copy out the form on page 7. Fill in the form as you read each answer.

Examiner's questions

These are some of the questions that the examiner will ask while reading the answers:

Answer A	Answer B
1 *Does it describe the place well?*	**1** *Does it describe the place well?*
2 *Is it well organised?*	**2** *Is it well organised?*
3 *Are the sentences clear and is the grammar correct?*	**3** *Are the sentences clear and is the grammar correct?*
4 *Are the sentences properly punctuated?*	**4** *Are the sentences properly punctuated?*
5 *Does the writer use words well and spell them correctly?*	**5** *Does the writer use words well and spell them correctly?*
6 *What grade would you give this piece of writing?*	**6** *What grade would you give this piece of writing?*

Answer A

I am writting this letter because I am
doing a serious called 'Snapshot' I was
wouldring after I have finshed it all if you
would put it in you newspaper for your local
5 compertensine.

I am going to write about my village. It is
quite a nice place. Has I walk outside my
house I have a street view of a lot of
houses a car park and some tress.

10 Has I walk on further down we have the
council offers which use to be any old
church has I walk further on thought the
village we have about six shops then just
across from the shops we have a little
15 park. We have no factory or big buildings
around us. This is a small village all we
have is about four hundred houses on the
whole estate I think that the whole estate
is quite small and not many people live up
20 there.

I think that my village is a very nice place
to live and I like liveing up there.

Answer B

The park is central to life in the town. It is the place where babies are taken for their first ride in a pushchair, where children spend their summer playing on the swings, where boyfriends meet their 5 girlfriends for romantic walks, where married couples take their families for picnics and where the elderly let their afternoons pass by, feeding the ducks. It can be a haven of peace and quiet, with its lush green fields, crystal-clear ponds and yellow 10 daffodils in spring, or it can be a vibrant centre of activity where children play noisily, where the local football and tennis matches are held, and where avid cyclists test out new mountain-biking techniques.

15 Its huge iron gates look forbidding but open up to reveal a welcoming place full of warmth and life. It is a place of happiness and of innocent pleasures, with seemingly hundreds of trees adding a certain charm and air. The beautiful landscaped gardens, 20 brimming with flowers of every description, are a myriad of colour in spring and summer while the extensive play area offers the child's dream and attracts children from all the surrounding estates. There is a part of the park for everyone.

25 The park is one of those places full of the little moments where life is relaxed, happy and carefree.

What a teacher thinks

This is how a teacher answered the questions on the form on page 7:

Answer A

1 ***Does it describe the place well?*** The writer doesn't really know how to begin. The answer doesn't start until the second paragraph – you could miss out the first paragraph completely and nothing would be lost. Then she tries to cover too much and doesn't describe anything very well. It's a pity she didn't choose just one or two things and describe them in more detail.	There is more about how to tackle questions in Chapter 2.
2 ***Is it well organised?*** No. It is very simple and there is no real shape to it. She should have made a plan before she started writing.	There is more about how to organise your writing in Chapter 2.
3 ***Are the sentences clear and is the grammar correct?*** No. There are many mistakes. Look at the first sentence in the third paragraph (lines 10–15) – it is really two sentences written as one. The last sentence in that paragraph (lines 16–20) is three sentences written as one!	There is more about sentences and grammar in Chapter 3.
4 ***Are the sentences properly punctuated?*** No. For example, the first and last sentences in paragraph 3 (lines 10–15 and 16–20) should be split up using full stops and capital letters. The second sentence in paragraph 2 (lines 7–9) contains a list and the items in it should be separated by commas.	There is more about punctuation in Chapter 4.
5 ***Does the writer use words well and spell them correctly?*** There are many simple spelling mistakes: 'serious' for 'series' (line 2) , 'has' for 'as' (line 7), 'tress' for 'trees' (line 9) , 'offers' for 'office' (line 11) and so on.	There is more about words and spelling in Chapter 5.
6 ***What grade would you give this piece of writing?*** F	

Answer B

1 ***Does it describe the place well?***

Yes. The writer has clearly thought carefully about the park and imagined it well. There are lots of details that help the reader see what she is describing. Also she makes good contrasts (young and old people, lively activities and quiet, for example). These give the writing life and variety.

2 ***Is it well organised?***

Yes. It isn't particularly complicated, but it moves easily from one topic to the next and is easy to follow. Paragraph 1 is about people who go to the park and how they use it. Paragraph 2 gives an impression of what the park is like without people. Paragraph 3 sums it up.

3 ***Are the sentences clear and is the grammar correct?***

Yes. There are short and long sentences. All are grammatically correct and well constructed.

4 ***Are the sentences properly punctuated?***

Yes. The writer knows exactly what she is doing.

5 ***Does the writer use words well and spell them correctly?***

The writer has a wide vocabulary. For example she uses words like 'haven' (line 8), 'crystal-clear' (line 9), 'avid' (line 13) and 'myriad' (line 21). Spelling is very accurate.

6 ***What grade would you give this piece of writing?***

A

Check with the examiner

Look on page 139 to see what the examiner wrote about these two answers.

On the next three pages are three exam answers. The writers were asked to describe the scene in a supermarket on a Saturday morning.

1 Read each one carefully.
2 For each one answer questions 1-5 on page 7.
3 What are the strengths and the weaknesses of each answer?
4 Decide on the order in which you would place them: which is the best and which is the least good?
5 What grade would you give each one?

Answer C

The door screamed open and more shoppers eagerly tried to
push themselves into the already overcrowded store. Ageing
trolleys squeaked their way between the ~~isles~~ aisles as bleary
eyed parents tried to pull their young children away from the
5 colourful temptation of the sweet counter. Shop assistants
were refilling the rapidly emptying shelves ~~and~~ as people
squeezed past to reach their favourite brands.

Saturday morning was always the busiest time of the week.
The workers on the checkout hated Saturday because they
10 always had so many people to serve. Regularly, they would be
~~m~~ running the items along the checkout, trying their hardest to
shorten the long queues, but someone would always complain
that they were working too slowly.

It was also so noisy. The tasteful relaxing music in the
15 background which flowed out from the speakers around the
store, was drowned by a wave of young children screaming, the
sound of metal attacking metal, the monotonous beeps of the
tills and the groaning shoppers. ~~People~~ Some people would
bring their whole family to help with the weekly groceries, and
20 were helplessly trying to control their excited young children.

The shoppers in the store were all so varied. There were
families, the young and the old, but they were all brought
together by the ~~strength of~~ necessity of shopping. The struggle
and exhaustion the shoppers all went through was caused
25 by the influence of commercialism, dictating where they
should shop and what they should buy. Without even realising
it, these people were the victims of a carefully controlled
society where people believed they had choice, but in reality,
they had none. Every Saturday was the same.

Answer D

A tipycal ~~se~~ scene in a supermarket ~~se~~ on a Saturday
morning is awful as their is a lot of people shopper as
they couldn't last week because they were working.

When you first walk in to a supermarket you ~~ort~~
5 automatically get a trolley and start to shop, After a
while you either forget what your want or they just have
not could what you need.

Your in the supermarket for ages because you crushed
together like a sandwich. you can't get out. But after a
10 while you manage to wriggle out and go and get more
~~supples~~ supplys and ~~is~~ then ~~on~~ the ~~queae~~ que for
ages as their is only one person on the tills

When you do get served and packed all your food,
vegatables, etc you just want to go home and relax. But
15 you can't as you have to ~~up~~ unpack the shopping and
make it neat within the cupboards, and then you can sit
down with a cup of tea and relax to watch the ~~tv~~
television.

Answer E

The supermarket car park is full you drive down each and every lane to find a space untill you find someone trying to leave and you wait.

Now you begin to walk to the supermarket dodging reversing 5 *cars you pass through the automatic doors and take one of the last but three trollies remaining as you walk inside. You first of all look towards the fruit and vegetables and see that the only apples left are the brused ones; you get all you can all the same. You pass through the supermarket isle by isle looking for all the* 10 *bargains and proceed towards the dairy section. You find that the only milk left is the bottles that expire tommorrow so you continue to the meat counter you find that the only piece of beef they have left is the sort you didn't like last time. As you walk towards the alcoholic section you find several middle aged men* 15 *with large guts filling their trollies with whatever they can find.*

The final and the worst part the paying. You stand in a line waiting for the akward person in front of you to pay by credit card and that also wants cash back you finally get to the till and find you have several items without a barcode and you have to 20 *wait for as the assistant manager to fiddle around with the computer alot. You finally get to leave. Someone who is not looking where they are going rams you in the back with a trolley and says sorry, as you walk off in screaming agony as you load your car boot and finally leave the supermarket.*

Check: *Now turn to page 143 and check your answers against the examiner's response.*

Your own writing

Look at some pieces of your own writing which have been marked and graded by your teacher. Apply the **Examiner's questions** on page 7 to your own writing. Can you see why it has been given the grade it has? How might your answer be improved? Is your writing weaker in some areas than others? If so, you may wish to concentrate on a particular chapter in this book.

Organising your writing

This chapter looks at the way you organise and present your writing. It focuses particularly on non-fiction writing:

- *descriptions*
- *arguments*
- *reports*
- *letters.*

By the time you have finished working through the chapter you should be able to:

✓ think clearly about your audience and know how to write for them
✓ think clearly about **why** you are writing and plan accordingly
✓ research and prepare your writing more effectively
✓ know how to redraft your writing (especially useful for coursework)
✓ check your writing carefully and systematically.

Contents

Read the question! 16
This section looks at the different kinds of question you may face

Why am I writing this? 17
This section explains how you should think about the audience *and the* purpose *of your writing*

Age alert 18

Don't get too personal! 19
This looks at how you should change the way you write according to the audience you are writing for

Don't panic! 21
This introduces a practical way of working when writing for the exam

Think 22

Plan it! 23
These sections show you how to generate ideas and plan for your writing

Starting to write 26
This concentrates on writing the first draft

Check it 28
How to check and redraft your work

Read the question!

Here are seven exam questions:

1

Design a one-page handout for ten-year-old children to make them aware of environmental issues.

2

Write a letter to the Environmental Department of your local council, setting out ways it could improve your local environment.

3

'All parents should be worried about the effect of television on their children.'
What do you think about this statement and what would you say to parents who are worried?
You could comment on:

- the violence you see on television
- spending too much time in front of the television, especially late at night
- being influenced by the commercials.

4

Write a set of rules for your class which could be agreed by the teacher and pupils and say why you have chosen them.

5

Write a dialogue between a teacher and a pupil who have disagreed over the interpretation of a school rule.

6

Write a conversation between a parent and a teenager who differ in their views about what the teenager should do on leaving school. Set the scene and make their different viewpoints clear.

7

During the last year you will have been through the process of deciding what to do after you finish compulsory schooling. You may have decided to stay at school, go to a local college or look for training or a job.
Write a lively article for your school magazine which you think would be helpful to next year's leavers when they are faced with the same decisions.
You could use the headline 'Is there life after school?' or you could provide your own. Think carefully about the way you set out your article.
The quality of your writing is more important than its length.

1 Which one of these exam questions do you think you could answer best? Why?

2 Which one of these questions do you think you might find the most difficult? Why?

3 In which questions do the examiners give advice on how you should write? What advice do they give?

Check: *Now turn to page 144 to check your answer to self-test question 3.*

Why am I writing this?

Before you start writing – or even planning to write – ask yourself the questions on this page.

Unless you think carefully about your **audience**, you cannot communicate properly with them.

Ask yourself:

- How much does my audience know about this subject?
- Do I need to begin by explaining things? If so, what?
- Are there any reasons why I should write in simple language? (For example, are my readers young children who cannot read very well yet?)
- Should I be careful not to use complicated words and sentences for these readers?
- How well do I know them? How friendly or relaxed can I be in the way I write?
- Do I need to be careful not to offend them by being too relaxed?

Unless you know the **purpose** of your writing, you will not be able to express yourself clearly and your audience will lose track of your ideas. You will often find that your writing has more than one purpose.

Your purpose might be:

- To entertain
- To give information
- To put across a point of view
- To explain my opinion
- To explain how something works
- To describe what something or someone looks like
- To set out rules and regulations
- To keep in touch with someone I know.

1 Look back at exam question **1** on page 16. Who is the audience for the handout?

2 What is its purpose?

3 Look at the other exam questions and write down the audience and purpose for each.

***Check:** Now check your answers on page 144.*

Age alert

Think about *how* you would write the same story for adults and for young children. Let's look at a well known children's story as an example. If you were telling **Goldilocks and the Three Bears** to a young child, it might begin like this:

> Once upon a time, there was a girl with long golden hair. Her name was Goldilocks. She lived near a forest. One morning she went for a walk in the forest ...

The language is simple, the sentences are not too complicated. Young children would be able to follow it.

If you were to write the same story for adults, it could be very different:

> They called her Goldilocks, Goldie for short. You could see why the moment you met her. Her hair! Men would stand and stare open-mouthed when she walked down the street. Goldie never let it bother her. She knew what she wanted in life and she was not going to let other people's prejudices get in her way. She hated the dumb blonde tag so she kept herself to herself. One morning ...

Writing practice

Write two versions of the opening few sentences of a story you know well:

- for children
- for adults.

You can choose any storyline you wish. You could try another fairy tale such as **Jack and the Beanstalk** or **Cinderella**. Alternatively, you could use the storyline from a soap that you watch. Think about your readers:

- How old are they?
- How much do they know?
- What style do they expect?
- Will my writing bore them?
- Will my writing offend them?

Don't get too personal!

When you are writing for an adult whom you have never met, it is a mistake to write too personally - especially if your audience is someone important. In the answers which follow, students were writing to their local Member of Parliament. They were expressing their concern about the damage being caused to Brazil and to its people by the destruction of the rainforests. They had read an appeal by Friends of the Earth and were using that advertisement as their source of information.

Look first at the opening words of this letter:

1

Dear MP,
I have joined the Friends of the Earth to help stop the evil mahogany trade. How can you let this go on? So many innocent Indians and their children have been killed just for the sake of mahogany trees.

An examiner comments

When we speak, or write, to a particular audience, we adjust our tone and vocabulary. We do not speak in the same way to our friends as we do to the headteacher. Most of the time we change instinctively.

The above writer is addressing a Member of Parliament and needs to use a formal style of address. She is very emotional about the issue and gets carried away and becomes rather rude and aggressive.

Being more formal

The letter above needed to be more formal. That is easier said than done. When students try to write more formally, it does not always work. Often they make their letter or article more complicated by using long words and long sentences. Frequently, it ends up sounding not quite right, as in this letter:

2

Dear Mr Jones,
I am writing to you in a disgusted and appalled state of mind which has been brought about by an advertisement that I have read from a newspaper regarding the Amazonian. I feel that something should be done about this matter and that everyone should know about the appalling scandal.

Getting better

You have looked at two pieces of writing that were not quite right for the intended audience. Finally, the following candidate gets closer to the right tone for this audience:

4

Dear Mr Jones,

I am writing to bring to your attention the evil trade in mahogany from the Amazon rainforest. This scandal has resulted in the murders of many native Indians, simply because of the West's greed for mahogany.

An examiner comments

This is a very confident and accomplished letter. It is clear what the subject is and how the writer feels. Equally important is the fact that the writer has not launched a personal attack on the M.P. It is the issue that matters most in this kind of writing, not the person.

SELF TEST

Look again at exam questions **1–7** on page 16. Some of these require a more formal style of writing than the others. Think about this and then put them in order, with the least formal at the beginning down to the most formal at the end.

***Check:** Now check your answer on page 144.*

Writing practice

Look at exam questions **1** and **2** on page 16. They are both about the environment, but they are addressed to very different audiences. Think about how you would start each piece of writing and then write an introductory paragraph for each of them.

Don't panic!

When you have read the question, what do you write?

Before you write you need to:

STOP ... THINK ... PLAN ... WRITE ... CHECK

Here are three good reasons to stop:

1 If you hurry, you often use even more time because you may have to rewrite.
2 If you stop to think, you don't write unnecessary things. Answers can be better and shorter!
3 If you stop to think, you can come up with original ideas and get higher marks.

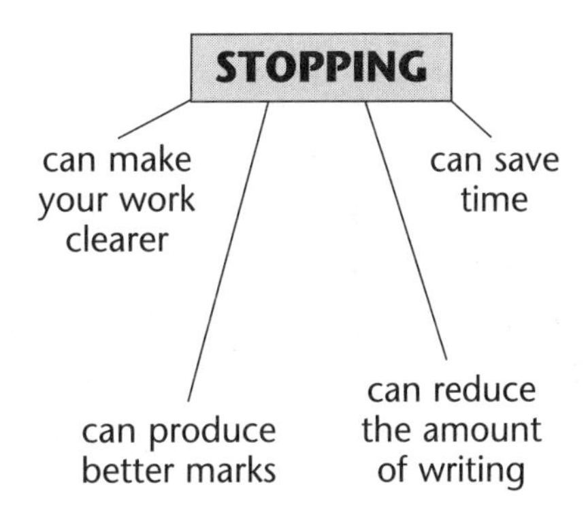

Think back over your last three or four written assignments (in any subjects). Ask yourself:

1 Was I well prepared when I started writing?
2 Did I hurry the work?
3 Did I get stuck part way through?
4 Was my grade/mark as high as it could have been?

Most people are full of ideas - until they need one. Then their mind goes blank. That's bad enough in ordinary life. In an examination, it can be a disaster.

Examination boards are not trying to catch you out. That is why you will often be given material that helps you generate ideas. Make the best use of it.

Write it down

Some people try to do all the thinking in their head. It helps a great deal to write a few words down. Writing things down means you don't forget ideas, especially if there is a chance of being interrupted. It also allows you to step back from an idea. Things that seem good in your head sometimes look different when you put them on paper. Test your thoughts by writing them down.

Writing practice

The writing practice in the next part of this chapter is all based on an exam question you have already seen (number 3 on page 16):

'All parents should be worried about the effect of television on their children'.

What do you think about this statement and what would you say to parents who are worried?

You could comment on:

- *the violence you see on television*
- *spending too much time in front of the television, especially late at night*
- *being influenced by the commercials.*

Notice that the question gives you three points to **think** about. Make a list of the ideas/thoughts that spring to mind on each of them. Do not spend more than five minutes on this. Keep the list for later in this chapter.

Thinking on paper is called planning. It needn't take long, but it:

- helps you think of more ideas
- helps you see the connections between them
- puts things in the right order
- helps you write faster because you know what to say.

Planning with lists

Lists are the simplest way to note ideas when you are planning to write. In an examination, that list may be in your head. However, if you can put your list on paper, you will guarantee your ideas are not forgotten. This is a list of points about the possible effects of television on family life:

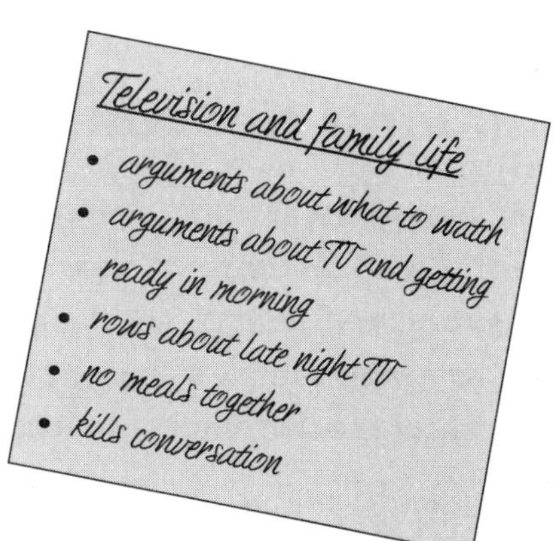

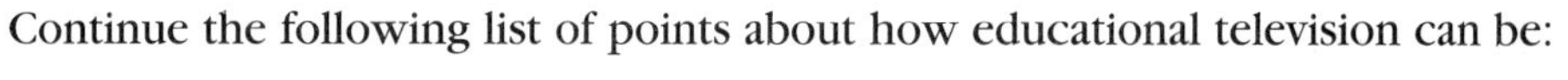

Writing practice

Continue the following list of points about how educational television can be:

Television and education

- *wildlife progs – can see things for science you couldn't see otherwise*

Planning with columns

Often, there are two sides to an argument. Making notes about both sides of an issue can be done in two columns. This example looks at the good and bad sides of television advertising:

Television commercials

For	Against
• informative	• see what you can't afford
• know what's available	• makes people buy what they don't need
• gives choice	• makes people envy other people
• no one has to buy	• things don't live up to their adverts
• entertaining	

Writing practice

Write your own notes for and against television soaps. You could begin like this:

For	*Against*
helps explain problems (e.g. parents splitting up)	

Planning the connections

Sometimes you will want to show the possible connections between several parts of a subject. This is often done with a web diagram (also called a spider diagram). These diagrams are especially useful when you are not sure where you are going to start and finish a subject. You can tick off each part of the diagram as you use it and then see what you have left.

The following simple example covers some points about violence on television:

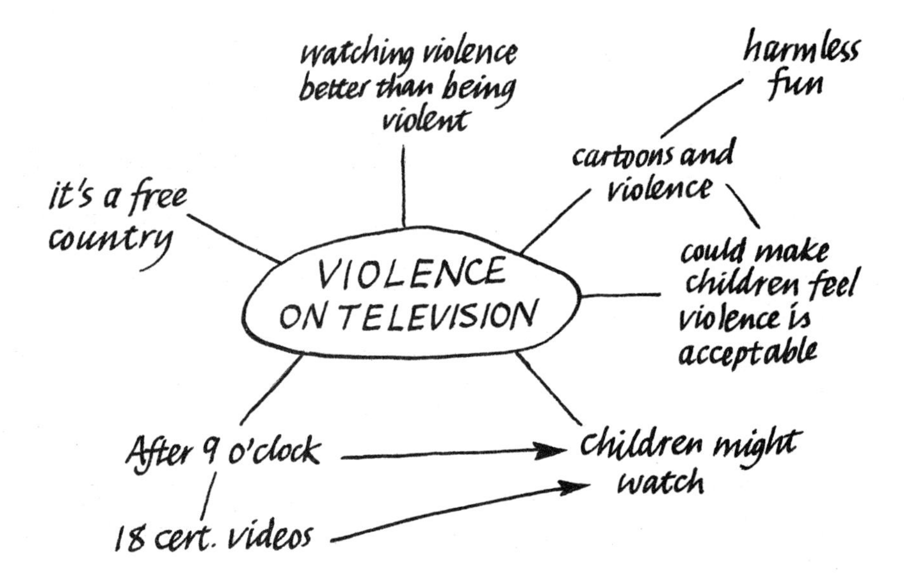

Writing practice

Try producing your own web diagram about violence and television. You can use some of the points suggested above but also add ideas of your own.

Planning for coursework

In an examination, you have to plan quickly. For coursework, you have more time. Most people waste it. Don't! You need to:

- Start early.
- Use any available computer facilities.
- Find out what videos or audio cassettes there are on the subject.
- Most of all, make the best possible use of books.

The following two diagrams should help you:

Finding books

Local library
Catalogue
Right section
Books not found
Books found
Librarian
Books found
Books not found
Central library
(or bigger branch library)
Librarian
Books found
Books not found
Go back to person who set work

Using available books

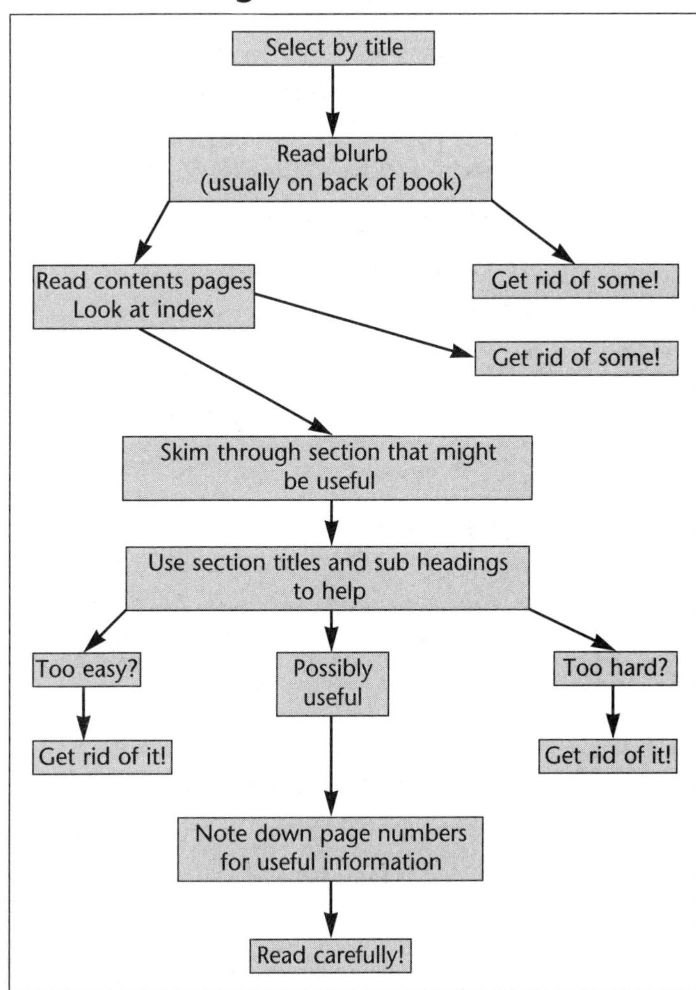

Book look

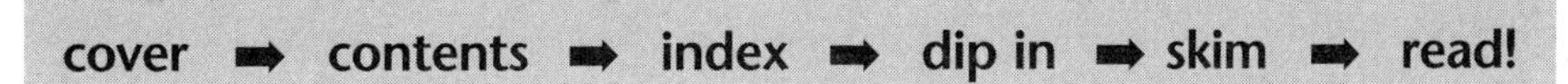

Planning can take several hours for coursework or just minutes in an examination. Either way, the moment comes when you have to put something on paper. This is the make or break moment.

An example

Here are two examination answers to question 7 on page 16.

1 Read Answer **A**.
2 As you read it, make notes on what you think of the way it is written. Refer back to the form on page 7 to help you. In place of question 1, you could ask, 'Does it deal with the subject well?'
3 Then do the same with Answer **B**.

Answer A

<u>Life After School</u>

Have you ever thought about what you could do after school?
Well, the exams are getting near, and you had better be thinking.
Here are some choices that you can choose from:
<u>Stay on at school</u>
5 *Here you will stay on and go to the sixth form at your school, if not another. This*
will help to give you A levels and may be you'll go onto university where, if you're a
swot, you can get a masters degree on the subjects you choose.
<u>Go to a local college</u>
This is very similar to the sixth form except you don't have to go to school
10 *everyday. There are some specialised colleges for agriculture, engineering and many*
more. You can achieve the same grades as A levels and again go onto university.
<u>Get a job, get some money</u>
If you can't get the grades to go to the sixth form or college then get a job and
start from there to work your way up the career, for example you may work as a
15 *waiter and then a few years become a head waiter.*
Well, its up to you to make a choice but always try your best and you will succeed.

Answer B

Is there life after sixteen?

It seems a long way off to you now, but you've got to make some serious choices. A job? College? Stay at school? Even if you decide which one is best for you, finding the right path can be a nightmare, but it needn't be.

5 Think of what you enjoy. It's no use spending your life doing something you hate. Don't be afraid if you don't follow the crowd – everyone has their interests and it's up to you to prove how well you can do.

The second thing is that you don't need to push yourself too far. Work with what you are comfortable with – there are no marks for struggling

10 and failing at the end of it all. The outside world may seem daunting but there's a lot that life has to offer, as long as you make the right decision.

You can never predict the future. You will never know what life has in store. But it's up to you to do what you want to do, not your friends, not your family, not anyone else but you.

SELF TEST

Read through the notes you have made. Make sure that you have commented on all the important points for each answer.

Check: *Now check your comments against those of the examiner on page 145.*

Writing practice

Parts of Answer **A** are badly expressed.

1 Look carefully at the following sentence and work out what is wrong with it.

2 Re-write it in better English.

If you can't get the grades to go to the sixth form or college then get a job and start from there to work your way up the career, for example you may work as a waiter and then a few years become a head waiter.

Writing practice

As you worked through this chapter, you made notes for an answer to the question on page 16 about watching television. Now you are going to write the whole piece.

1 Read through all the notes you have made so far.
2 Look again at question **3** on page 16. Have you missed out any important points that should be included? If so, add them to your notes.
3 Look at all the notes you have made. Ask yourself: what are the main points I want to cover? (There should be three, four or five points.)
4 Work out the best order to tackle them. Take a fresh piece of rough paper and write the points in that order, with plenty of space between them.
5 Look through the rest of the notes and work out how each of them can be linked to one of your main points. Write each one under the main point it is linked to.
6 Think of a good way to start.
7 Think of a good way to finish.
8 Now write your answer.

Once you have written your answer, make sure it does what it set out to do.

Check the flow

A basic question is whether an answer reads fluently. With coursework, some students find it helpful to read work aloud to get a sense of how it sounds. You cannot do that in examinations but it is possible to imagine you are reading it aloud whilst going through it silently. That is why you will often see exam candidates' lips moving and no sound coming out! They are checking their work and trying to hear what it sounds like inside their head. It sounds odd but it can work. Try it first before you reach your actual examinations.

Writing practice

Check the flow now for the piece you have just written.
Make any changes you think are necessary.

Check the relevance

Your answer must be relevant. That means it actually answers the question that was set, not the question you would have liked!

Ask yourself:

1 What have I missed out that ought to be there?
2 What have I added in that I do not need?
3 Is it right for the audience?

Writing practice

- Ask yourself these three questions about the piece you have just written.
- Make a note of any changes you think are necessary.

Check the paragraphing

People in a hurry tend to forget paragraphs. You have time to put this right in coursework, but not in examinations. You need to try to get it right first time.

The theory is simple. New subjects require new paragraphs. Putting it into practice is not so straightforward. When is a subject new? Some subjects may be too long for one paragraph and need to be broken down into two or more sections. Sometimes work can flow so smoothly that it is difficult to see where the paragraph should break.

There is more about paragraphing on pages 53–57 and 74.

Writing practice

- Read through the piece you have just written.
- Make sure that it is properly divided into paragraphs.
- If you have two paragraphs where there should only be one, mark a link between them, like this: 
- If you have a paragraph that should be split, mark the start and write n.p. in the margin.

Check for punctuation

Make sure that sentences make sense, beginning with a capital letter and ending with a full stop. Nearly everyone can do it, but sentences often break down under pressure. Look carefully at any sections where you have used speech marks or apostrophes.

There is more about punctuation starting on page 59.

Writing practice

- Check your punctuation now on the piece you have just written.
- Make any changes you think are necessary.

Check your spelling

On a word processor take advantage of any spell-checking system but do not rely on it - it can produce very strange results. If you know you have particular weaknesses, look out for them.

There is more about checking spelling, starting on page 100.

Writing practice

- Check your spelling now on the piece you have just written.
- Make any changes you think are necessary.

Check your presentation

Watch your handwriting at all times. It is no good writing in a hurry if what you write cannot be read. Every now and then, stand back from your work. Ask yourself if other people would really want to take a look at what you are presenting. If you are unhappy with what you see, do what you can to make the layout clearer and more accessible.

Writing practice

- Look again at the piece you have just written.
- Make any changes to presentation you think are necessary.

Writing practice

Unless you are a very good writer indeed, you should have made a number of corrections to your piece of writing, and notes about how it should be improved. Re-write it so that all these improvements are included in the final version.

Sentences and paragraphs

Many people have problems with constructing sentences that are accurate and informative. If candidates for GCSE write sentences that are ungrammatical they lose marks. But how do you avoid making mistakes in the first place? How do you learn how to write better sentences and paragraphs?

You do not have to be a grammar expert to write well, but it helps if you have a basic understanding of how sentences are constructed and if you know some of the words that are used to describe different grammatical features.

This chapter contains the information you need. It introduces technical terms as you go along. These are also listed on page 128 onwards - look there if you come across a word you do not understand.

Grammar is a set of explanations of how our language works. It tells us:

- How words are arranged into short and long sentences. This is called **syntax**.
- How words are changed according to where they come in a sentence and how they are being used. This is called **morphology**.
- How whole texts are organised.

Contents

Different kinds of sentence 33
How simple sentences work 34
These sections help you make sure that the sentences you write are grammatically correct
The subject 34
The verb 36
The verb phrase 38
Checking agreement 40
Getting the tense right 42
Is the verb complete? 44
These describe the grammatical terms you need in order to understand how sentences are constructed
Simple sentences 46
Multiple sentences 46
Compound sentences 48
Complex sentences 49
Different ways of building up short and long sentences that are clear and effective
Paragraphs 53
How to construct clear and interesting paragraphs

Different kinds of sentence

You can write sentences for four different purposes:

1 **To make a statement:**
Peter hates chocolate.
It is only since going to Brackley School that I have enjoyed playing netball.

2 **To ask a question:**
What's the time?
Is it true that you're going out with Deirdre Witherspoon?

3 **To order, command, or request:**
Don't do that!
Please do not stick used chewing gum underneath the desks.
These are called **directives**.

4 **To exclaim:**
How fortunate it is that we met!
What a ridiculous person Peter is!
Although exclamations are followed by an exclamation mark, not all sentences that have them are exclamations. Directives often end with an exclamation mark.

Statement sentences

Most of the sentences you write are statements, so this chapter focuses on statement sentences.

Say what type of sentence each of these is:

1 Are you the only person in the class who brought their stereo to school today?
2 Students should not leave personal property in the classroom.
3 Don't leave your belongings in school overnight!
4 How am I supposed to know where you left your stereo?
5 How fortunate you are that the caretaker found it!

Check: *Now check your answers on page 146.*

How simple sentences work

In the first part of this chapter you look at the commonest ways in which simple sentences can go wrong. (Don't worry if you don't know what a 'simple' sentence is yet - you soon will.)

All statement sentences must have a subject and a verb. Most of the problems people have with sentences involve these two parts of a sentence. If you can identify the subject and the verb in your own sentences and then make a few simple checks, you are well on the way to writing accurately and correctly.

The subject

Every statement sentence has a subject.

Position

1 The subject usually comes before the verb. It is often the first part of the sentence:

__Elaine__ has been working well in chemistry lessons.
__Jason's problems with mathematics__ affect his work in physics.

2 Sometimes the subject doesn't come right at the beginning of the sentence:

This term, __Elaine__ has been working well in chemistry lessons.

3 Very occasionally you find sentences where the subject does not come before the verb:

There in the corner stood __a handsome stranger__.

Meaning

The subject usually tells us what or who the sentence is going to be about. The sentences above tell us about Elaine, and about Jason's problems with mathematics. Sometimes sentences have a subject that does not give such direct information but tells the reader to wait for what comes next:

***It** was a beautiful summer's day.* ***There** have been serious robberies nearby.*

But the subject still comes before the verb and again it is often the first thing in the sentence.

How many words?

The subject can be one word or a group of words called a **phrase**.

SELF TEST

What is the subject of each of these sentences?

1 It was a still hot day in June.
2 Everybody else in the family had gone into town to do the shopping.
3 Sarah was still in bed.
4 After lying in bed for another half an hour, she decided to have some breakfast.
5 Unfortunately the cereal packet was empty.
6 The bread bin was empty, too.
7 There was nothing to eat.

Check: *Now check your answers on page 146.*

Writing practice

In each of these sentences there is a blank instead of a subject. Write out the sentences, adding a subject that will fit the rest of the sentence.

Craftsman, David Cubbage, is reviving a centuries' old skill to kit out modern-day knights in shining armour. ...., aged 48, who is based at Norton, near Gloucester, makes made-to-measure suits of armour for Britain's military re-enactment groups. .... has also been bought by film producers, museums and owners of medieval castles.

'......... is a very difficult trade to learn because nothing was ever written down,' he said. '......... was a closely guarded secret so consequently we have had to learn from scratch.'

.... belongs to a Gloucestershire-based re-enactment group called the Companions of the Black Bear who relive the Battle of Tewkesbury on the anniversary of the 1471 battle.

'......... joined the group in 1986 and needed a suit of armour and I could not afford to buy one so I decided to make it myself,' he said. 'Recently .... got made redundant as an instructor for an engineering company and I was offered a workshop at the Ronsons reclamation yard in Norton.'

.... is one of a handful of full-time armouries in the country.

The verb

Every sentence must have a verb.

Position

1 In a statement sentence, the verb normally comes after the subject. It often comes immediately after the subject:

My little brother Sean | ***loves*** | *playing with the computer.*
← **subject** → | **verb** | ← **rest of sentence** →

2 Sometimes there are one or more words between the subject and the verb:

My older brother | *unfortunately* | ***lost*** | *his job yesterday.*
← **subject** → | | **verb** |

Meaning

The verb tells you about the subject and often links the subject with the rest of the sentence.

1 It can give information about an action:
*The three girls **were kicking** a small football along the pavement.*

2 It can give information about a state or condition:
*Those three girls **love** football.*

3 There is also a small group of verbs that just link the subject and the rest of the sentence. They work like the equals sign in a sum, because what comes before and after them refers to the same person or thing:
*My grannie **is** Scottish* → My grannie = Scottish
*The family **seems** very happy* → The family = very happy
Common **linking verbs** include *is*, *am*, *are*, *seem*, *appear* and *become*.

How many words?

The verb in a sentence can be one word (*loves*) or a group of words, a **verb phrase**. All the words in a verb phrase are themselves verbs. Sometimes verb phrases can be quite long:

*By now I **should have been being seen** by the doctor.*

SELF TEST

What is the verb or verb phrase in each of these sentences?

1 My favourite colour is blue.
2 You should be so lucky.
3 You should unwrap the cartridge carefully.
4 This time tomorrow we should be being driven round Paris in an open-top bus.
5 The players were depressed by the weather.
6 I should have thought so.
7 You have never been so unlucky.

Check: *Now check your answers on page 146.*

Writing practice

In this extract there are eight blanks where there should be verbs. At the bottom of the page there is a list of ten verbs. Choose a verb to fit each blank. Remember that there are more verbs in the list than you need, so make sure that you choose the right ones!

Life after the army

Larry Hollingworth describes how he came to work for the United Nations

I wanted travel and fun and a challenge. I .... away my razor, bequeathed most of my suits and ties to the local charity shop, ... a suitcase and visited Geneva. I .... to be an aid worker. Preferably with refugees. My overseas tours, especially those in Africa, and most memorably in Uganda, had .... me with a secret wish to go back and do something positive and permanent. What and where I did not know. I only .... it had to be with people.

Long ago I .... that I am a 'people person'. When friends .... from holidays and got out the photographs I was interested if they were of people. Photos of parks, beaches, trees and buildings don't draw my attention in the same way. But snaps of men fishing, women working and children playing fascinate me. I knew that I did not want to save jungles, mend the hole in the ozone layer or restore monuments. I wanted to work with people. Everybody wants to work with children, but I was more attracted to whole families, to whole communities. I had no idea of what I could do but I knew that I .... on my own in the middle of nowhere.

Verbs

believed could stand expected had discovered knew left
packed returned threw wanted

The verb phrase

The verb in a sentence can be one word or several.

Full verb

In a verb phrase there is always one word, the **full verb** which gives the meaning (the action or state). In these sentences, the verb phrase is *underlined*, and the full verb is in ***bold***:

*She has been **seeing** a lot of him recently.*
*I have never yet **visited** Manchester.*

Auxiliary verbs

If a verb phrase contains more than one word, it consists of a full verb and one or more auxiliary verbs. In the sentences above, the auxiliary verbs are 'has been' and 'have'. Auxiliary verbs work with the main verb to add further information. They are:

can/could   may/might   will/would   shall/should   must

Look at these pairs of sentences and see how the use of auxiliary verbs affects the meaning of the sentence:

*He often **goes** to football matches.*
*He should **go** less often.*

*I **read** thrillers.*
*I might **read** the newspaper today.*

Primary verbs

There are three verbs which can be used as main verbs or as auxiliaries:
is/am/be   have/had   do/did/does

1 **They can stand on their own in a sentence as a full verb:**

*She **is** happy.*
*Pollution **does** a lot of damage.*

2 **Or they can work with a full verb:**

*She is **going** home.*
*Pollution does **matter** a lot.*

The whole verb

When you are picking out the verb in a sentence, make sure you get the whole verb phrase. This can be complicated because other words may be slipped into the middle of a verb phrase:

We <u>are</u> at this very moment <u>eating</u> our breakfast.

For each of the following simple sentences, write down the whole verb phrase.

1 Maria is very keen on music.
2 She started to learn the piano five years ago.
3 Now she has reached Grade 5.
4 She ought to be able to pass it easily.
5 She hopes to continue her studies at the 6th Form College.

The rest of the sentences are multiple sentences. Write down **all** the verb phrases in each one.

6 When we finally reached the top of Snowdon it was snowing.
7 So we were unable to see the route by which we had ascended.
8 It would soon be getting dark, and we were anxious about getting back safely.
9 Fortunately just as things were looking serious, the weather began to break and we were able to follow the railway track back down the mountain.

Check: *Now check your answers on page 146.*

Checking agreement

Verbs change according to the subject. We say that the subject and the verb in a sentence must **agree**. The problem is that standard English and local dialects do this in different ways. This is how it works in standard English:

Subject	Verb			
	Walk	**Have**	**Be (Present)**	**Be (Past)**
I	walk	have	am	was
he/she/it	walks	has	is	was
we	walk	have	are	were
you	walk	have	are	were
they	walk	have	are	were

Dialect and standard English

In some local dialects people use expressions such as *we was*, *they be* and *she am*. These aren't wrong if you are speaking in dialect, but they are definitely wrong if you are writing standard English.

Long subjects

It is a common mistake to write a sentence in which the subject and the verb do not agree. It often happens when the subject is made up of two or more things joined by 'and':

Friends of the Earth and I was shocked ...
This should be: *Friends of the Earth and I were shocked ...*

This is the way to check agreement:

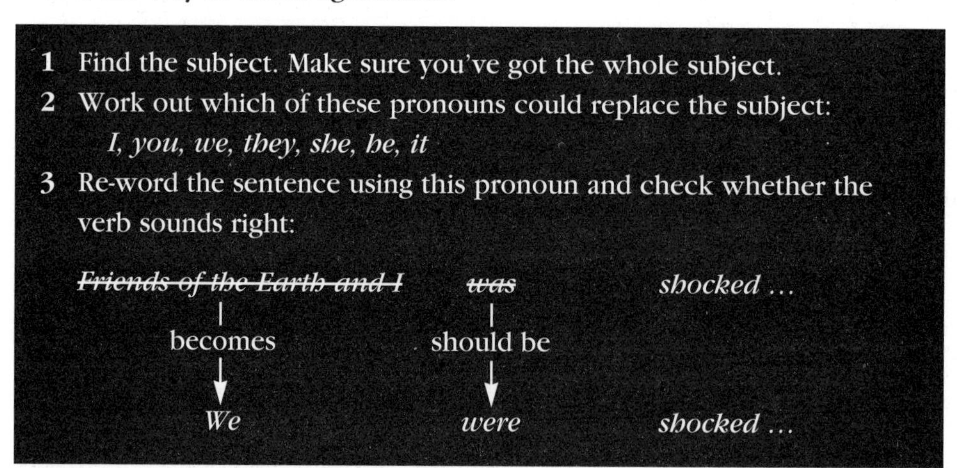

SELF TEST

In each of these sentences, which of the verbs in brackets is correct?

1 During last term, several of my friends and I (was/were) disappointed that we never played basketball.
2 In the cross-country Mary, limping in after most of the others, (was/were) 45th.
3 Collecting stamps (is/are) a popular hobby with retired postal workers.
4 The rules say that all those people who have lost an English book (have/has) to pay for another one.
5 At the party I saw a lot of my friends, including Janice and Shirley who (was/were) standing in a corner having a deep conversation.

Check: *Now check your answers on page 146.*

Writing practice

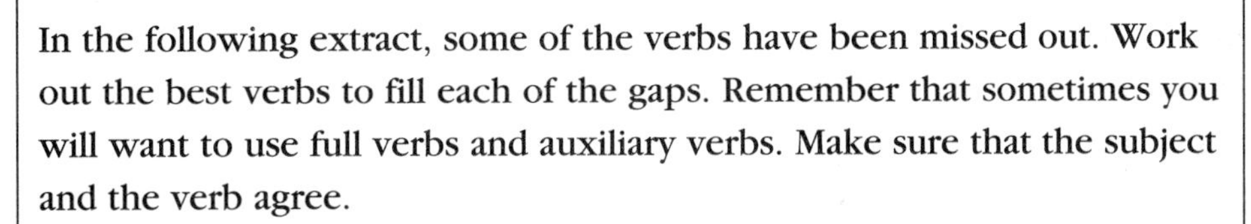

In the following extract, some of the verbs have been missed out. Work out the best verbs to fill each of the gaps. Remember that sometimes you will want to use full verbs and auxiliary verbs. Make sure that the subject and the verb agree.

Piers – a puppy with attitude

When Rumer Godden was 16 she was given £5 to buy a Persian kitten. Instead she bought a puppy.

In the pet shop there .... a rusty old bird cage and in it sat a puppy, small, square, black with cream paws and vest. He was of a kind I had not seen before but his eyes, which took up most of his face, ... at me compellingly. I bought him.

He was extraordinarily clever and extraordinarily brave. I had to go to school and he had necessarily to amuse himself through those long hours, which he did; one Saturday I took him to catch the bus up to the downs – buses were open topped then, and the conductor .... , 'is that your dog?'

'Yes.'

'Then you .... the Corporation at least ten pounds.'

It seemed Piers was in the habit of taking himself to the terminus and boarding the bus; he .... off at the Downs, spent the morning rabbiting and took the bus home. He was perfectly all right if people .... him alone but, often, seeing a small unaccompanied Pekingese, they took him to the police station and a bored policeman would have to come and tell Mam, 'Piers is in quod (prison) again.' It .... five shillings each time, but again I did not grudge it.

Getting the tense right

The verb in a sentence shows **when** something happened – past, present or future. This is called the verb tense. It is formed in two ways:

Changing the full verb

If the verb in the sentence is just a full verb, then it changes to show the tense:

PRESENT	*she* ***walks***	*they* ***speak***
PAST	*she* ***walked***	*they* ***spoke***

Using auxiliaries

1 We can use auxiliary verbs to make changes of tense:

FUTURE	*I* *shall* ***walk***	*she* *will* ***speak***

2 Sometimes when we use auxiliaries we have to change the form of the full verb as well:

PAST PERFECT	*I* *have* ***walked***	*she* *has* ***spoken***

Dozens of tenses

Overseas students trying to learn English often complain that it has far too many tenses! It certainly has far more than French or German, for example. These are different tenses of the verb *walk*:

she had walked
she has walked
she walked
she walks
she will walk
she will have walked
she had been walking
she has been walking
she was walking
she is walking
she will be walking
she will have been walking

Then there are these forms:

she used to walk
she was going to walk
she is going to walk

These words can also be used:

may/might/can/could/would/should/must

Check your tenses

When you are writing - especially telling stories - it is easy to mix your tenses. This kind of mistake is quite common. In this extract from a GCSE paper, the writer is describing his brother's problems with getting and keeping a job:

> A few months later he tells me he quit. I was really mad and frustrated with him. It's hard to get a job these days and he goes and throws one away. He said they treated him like dirt.

As you can see, this jumps from the present tense (*tells*) to the past (*was*) and back again. It should be:

> A few months later he told me he had quit. I was really mad and frustrated with him. It's hard to get a job these days and he went and threw one away. He said they treated him like dirt.

One verb has been left in the present, ***It's hard.*** Although the story takes place in the past, this sentence is telling us something that is still true (in the present) - ***It is hard to get a job.*** So the verb is in the present tense.

The story continues - the brother has got himself another job.
The verbs underlined are in the wrong tense. What should they be? The words with a ring round them are wrong too. Can you work out what they should be?

> (Now) a week ago he'<u>s said</u> he'<u>s given</u> it up. 'They treat me like dirt,' he <u>says</u> again. (Now) I was furious with him. He <u>has thrown</u> away two good jobs, two good jobs with fair pay.
> Many people would give their right arm for a job and he <u>throws</u> two away in two years. My mum doesn't know yet and when she finds out she is going to hit the roof, especially after two months ago he was voted 'Most Valuable Employee' at T.G.I. Friday's. That meant that he <u>has been working</u> hard and they <u>appreciate</u> it. He was also due for a pay rise as well. So quitting (now) was a stupid thing to do.

***Check:** Now check your answers on page 146.*

Is the verb complete?

A common error is to write a sentence that either has no verb at all, or only has part of the verb. A **complete sentence** must contain a **complete verb**.

Finite verbs

The technical term for a complete verb is a **finite verb**. A finite verb has to show two things:
- agreement with the subject
- tense.

When you are writing a piece that mixes storytelling and description it is easy to get carried away and miss out parts of the verb:

> *The car park is full with more cars still waiting for a space. Customers quickly grabbing a trolley despite its condition ...*

The second sentence has a subject *Customers*, but the verb *grabbing* is not complete. Verbs ending in *-ing* always need an auxiliary to complete them and make them into finite verbs. So the sentence should be re-written:

> *Customers quickly grab a trolley despite its condition ...*

Summary

To be complete, a statement sentence must have:

1. a **subject** that:
   - usually comes at or near the beginning
   - usually comes before the verb
   - can be one word or a phrase
   - usually tells the reader what the sentence is going to be about.
2. a **finite verb** that:
   - usually comes after the subject
   - tells the reader about an action or state (or is a linking verb)
   - can be one word or a verb phrase
   - agrees with the subject
   - shows the correct tense.

SELF TEST

Some of these sentences are incorrect. Which are they and how should they be re-written? Note: not all of them are wrong!

1 Most of the customers flock towards the bakery section.
2 Racing for the fresh bread just coming out of the ovens.
3 Trolleys whizzing up and down the aisles.
4 Children crying for a sweetie.
5 Later in the morning checkouts begin to fill with customers.
6 Customers fill their shopping bags, trying to keep up with the pace of the checkout staff.

Check: *Now check your answers on page 146.*

Writing practice

This is part of a set of notes a student made while watching a video. Turn them into a series of correct sentences.

Ruud Gullit player/manager of Chelsea.
Chelsea playing Derby last Saturday.
Gullit on as sub.
After 12 mins tackled and hurt ankle.
Taken off on stretcher.
X-rayed.
At first doctors said it was torn ligaments.
Later X-ray revealed broken ankle.
Chelsea favourites for FA cup in six weeks' time.
Doubtful to be fit in time.

Simple and multiple sentences

So far we have been looking at only one kind of sentence. But in fact most people use many different kinds of sentence.

Simple sentences

Some sentences contain only one finite verb. For example:

	Beginning parts	Subject	Verb	End parts
1		Jonah	works	hard
2	In amongst all the rubbish on her desk	Miriam Havergal, the famous crime writer,	found	a folder crammed with paper covered in her spidery handwriting.

Sentences that only contain one finite verb are called **simple sentences**. This does not mean that they are necessarily short or simple in meaning, as the second sentence shows.

Multiple sentences

We often write sentences that contain more than one finite verb.

This sentence contains two finite verbs, so it can be split into two parts:

The scene in a supermarket on a busy Saturday morning is one that brings grief, despair and memories.

Part 1			Part 2		
Subject	Verb	Rest	Subject	Verb	Rest
The scene in a supermarket on a busy Saturday morning	*is*	*one*	*that*	*brings*	*grief, despair and memories.*

Clauses

Each part of a sentence is called a **clause**. A simple sentence contains one clause. A sentence that contains more than one clause is called a **multiple sentence**.

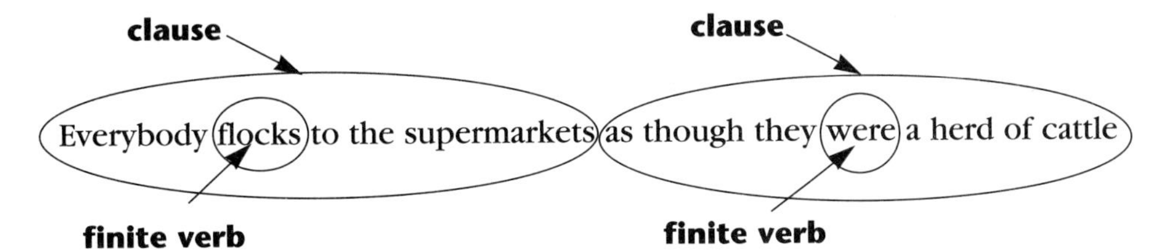

Remember that every clause must contain a finite verb.

Which of the following sentences are simple and which are multiple? The easiest way to check is to go through the sentences and pick out the finite verbs. Count the finite verbs in each sentence. If there is only one, it is a simple sentence. If there is more than one, it is a multiple sentence.

1 Ex-army cook Angela Sirdar was banned from joining the Royal Marines as a chef - because she is a woman.

2 And yesterday she went into battle to prove she is a victim of sex discrimination.

3 Angela, 31, became the first woman to challenge the marines' recruitment policy after being made redundant in 1995 following 11 years as a Royal Artillery chef.

4 She received a letter suggesting she apply to the marines, then found the invitation should have gone only to axed male cooks.

5 Angela, married to an ex-marine, was told women were barred from the elite force because EVERY one of its troops had to be able to fight in a war.

6 About £50 million in compensation has already been paid by the Ministry of Defence to women sacked by the armed forces after falling pregnant.

7 And the law now allows discrimination ONLY to ensure combat effectiveness.

Check: *Now check your answer on page 146.*

Compound sentences

There are many different ways in which we can join clauses to form multiple sentences. A very straightforward way of doing this is to join them with words like **and**:

Eddie didn't do much work for the exams.	+	*He got a Grade D for English.*	=	*Eddie didn't do much work for the exam* ***and*** *he got a Grade D for English.*

If we join clauses in this way, the sentences we make are called **compound sentences**.

Conjunctions

The words that are used to join sentences are called **conjunctions**. The conjunctions used to form compound sentences are:

but or nor then yet and

It makes a difference, of course, which conjunction you use. Imagine that you are talking to a pen-friend from Spain. How would you explain the difference in meaning between each of these groups of sentences?

1 **(a)** Eddie didn't do much work in the exams and he got a Grade D for English.
  (b) Eddie didn't do much work in the exams but he got a Grade D for English.

2 **(a)** Tomorrow I'm going swimming and I shall visit Donna.
  (b) Tomorrow I'm going swimming or I shall visit Donna.
  (c) Tomorrow I'm going swimming then I shall visit Donna.

3 **(a)** We went to the pictures in Poole but we walked home.
  (b) We went to the pictures in Poole then we walked home.
  (c) We went to the pictures in Poole and we walked home.

4 **(a)** She's sixteen yet she can drive a car.
  (b) She's sixteen or she can drive a car.
  (c) She's sixteen and she can drive a car.

Check: *Now check your answers on page 147.*

Complex sentences

The conjunctions used to form compound sentences do have different meanings. But compound sentences only give the reader a little more information than if we just wrote two simple sentences.

There are more complicated ways of joining two clauses. These two clauses can be combined in several different ways:

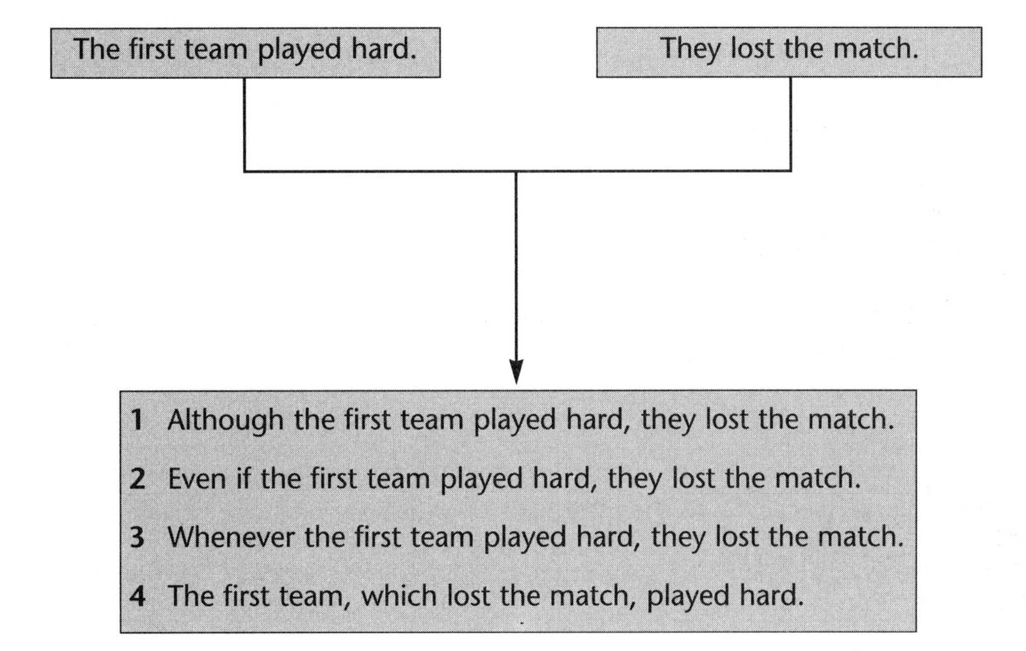

Sentences that link clauses in this way are called **complex sentences**.

Main clause

Each of the sentences above has one clause that will stand on its own.

1 They lost the match.
2 They lost the match.
3 They lost the match.
4 The first team played hard.

This clause is called the **main clause**.

Subordinate clause

The other clause in each sentence cannot stand on its own because it is incomplete.

1 Although the first team played hard …
2 Even if the first team played hard …
3 Whenever the first team played hard …
4 … which lost the match …

This clause is called the **subordinate clause**.

Writing practice

Each of the following pairs of simple sentences can be combined into one complex sentence, as was done in the examples on page 49. See how many different complex sentences you can make from each pair.

1 Sonya trained hard for the District Sports.
  She came second in the high jump.

2 It rains a lot in February.
  The football pitch cannot be used.

3 She works hard on her Saturday job.
  She earns £3 an hour.

4 I don't enjoy reading much.
  I like sci-fi stories.

5 Wayne is not very good at science.
  Wayne is an expert on computer games.

Good writing has a mix of simple and multiple sentences. What makes writing not just accurate and informative but interesting and entertaining is the way in which the writer chooses to do this.

When things go wrong

This is an extract from a GCSE paper:

> The picture is taken from a Michael Jackson concert. I was on stage when this accident occurred he was dancing to Billie Jean as he was attempting to moonwalk it didn't come off. 'Was this the end for Michael Jackson?' I asked myself but he eventually done in a wonderful style and finished the song. The crowd went wild they shouted, 'Michael, Michael, Michael,' etc. Then he came on again to do a couple more songs but in the song 'She's out of my life' you know when he collapses well he didn't collapse he threw himself onto the stage, everyone screamed in excitement but when he stood up his nose was all mashed up all over his face.

The second sentence is confused. If it is broken down into clauses we have:

1 I was on stage
2 this accident occurred
3 he was dancing to Billie Jean
4 he was attempting the moonwalk
5 it didn't come off

One way of joining the clauses would be like this:

> I was on stage when this accident occurred. As he was dancing to Billie Jean, he was attempting the moonwalk, but it didn't come off.

Re-write the last two sentences of the extract. These are the clauses:

1 the crowd went wild
2 they shouted, 'Michael, Michael, Michael'
3 he came on again to do a couple more songs
4 in the song 'She's out of my life' he collapses
5 he didn't collapse
6 he threw himself onto the stage
7 everyone screamed in excitement
8 he stood up
9 his nose was all mashed up all over his face

Check: *Now check your answer on page 147.*

Writing practice

This is a set of notes made from a television programme about the discovery of the tomb of Tutankhamun. Read them through and then follow the instructions at the end.

1 Archaeologist Howard Carter – financial backing from Lord Carnarvon
2 Went to Egypt several years running to search for tombs of Pharaohs
3 Concentrated on area known as the Valley of the Kings – near Luxor on the Nile
4 Little success
5 Lord Carnarvon agreed to one last expedition in 1922
6 A workman accidentally found stone staircase leading down – blocked up with rubble
7 Carter sent telegram to Lord Carnarvon telling him to come out as soon as possible
8 Carnarvon arrived – tomb opened
9 Tomb contained a mass of beautiful objects, many made of gold
10 A stone sarcophagus containing the body of Tutankhamun
11 Found no less than three coffins, one inside the next
12 Third coffin made of solid gold weighing over 100 kg
13 Took eight years to record, pack and remove all the contents of the tomb
14 Most of objects in Cairo Museum

This set of notes can be written up into a short text, containing four paragraphs:

A Howard Carter's early expeditions (notes 1–4)
B The 1922 expedition and the discovery of the tomb (notes 5–7)
C Opening the tomb (notes 8–12)
D The exploration of the tomb and its contents (notes 13–14)

The first paragraph could be written up like this:

The archaeologist Howard Carter, who had financial backing from Lord Carnarvon, went to Egypt several years running to search for the tombs of the Pharaohs. Carter concentrated on an area known as the Valley of the Kings – near Luxor on the Nile, but his efforts met with little success.

Now write the remaining three paragraphs in a similar way.

Paragraphs

If you are writing more than a few sentences, you need to divide your text into paragraphs. Writing in paragraphs has three main benefits:

Before you write, it makes you think about your text as a whole and the sections you want to divide it into.

You can't write paragraphs accurately unless you have at least made a rough plan of what you are going to say. If you want to, you can plan each paragraph in detail even before you start writing the first sentence.

As you are writng, it makes you think carefully about how your ideas are linked together and how to present them to the reader.

It helps readers find their way through the text.

Readers can, if they wish, pause at the end of a paragraph to think about it. They should be able to see how one idea leads to another. If they have to stop reading before the end, it is easier for them to find their place if the text is in paragraphs.

The key features of a paragraph

There are four key features of a paragraph, as illustrated by this examination answer.

1 Each paragraph is about a separate topic.

Paragraph 1
sets the scene

The door screamed open and more shoppers eagerly tried to push themselves into the already overcrowded store. Ageing trolleys squeaked their way between the aisles as bleary eyed parents tried to pull their young children away from the colourful temptation of the sweet counter. Shop assistants were refilling the rapidly emptying shelves as people squeezed past to reach their favourite brands.

Paragraph 2
tells us about the checkout workers' feelings

Saturday morning was always the busiest time of the week. The workers on the checkout hated Saturday because they always had so many people to serve. Regularly, they would be running the items along the checkout, trying their hardest to shorten the long queues, but someone would always complain that they were working too slowly.

Paragraph 3
describes how noisy it was

It was also so noisy. The tasteful relaxing music in the background which flowed out from the speakers around the store, was drowned by a wave of young children screaming, the sound of metal attacking metal, the monotonous beeps of the tills and the groaning shoppers. Some people would bring their whole family to help with the weekly groceries, and were helplessly trying to control their excited young children.

2 Each paragraph has a sentence or two at the beginning that tells us what it is about.

> *Saturday morning was always the busiest time of the week.*

3 Each paragraph builds on the ideas in the first one or two sentences by adding more details, new ideas or thoughts about the topic, or in some other way.

> *The workers on the checkout hated Saturday because they always had so many people to serve. Regularly, they would be running the items along the checkout, trying their hardest to shorten the long queues, but someone would always complain that they were working too slowly.*

4 Apart from Paragraph 1, each paragraph has a 'hook' at the beginning to link it to the previous paragraph.
Look at how the next paragraph begins:

> *It was also so noisy ...*

The word *also* tells us that this paragraph is **in addition to** what we have just read.

Paragraphs in a story

When you are writing a story, you should follow the same general guidelines, but there is one extra rule to remember:

In a story that contains direct speech (quoting the actual words spoken), you should start a new paragraph every time a new person speaks.

Summary

1 When you are planning, try to think in paragraphs.
2 When you are writing, think of each paragraph as a whole, with a beginning, a middle and an end.
3 Make sure that each paragraph leads neatly into the next, by placing 'hooks' in the right places.
4 Remember the rule about direct speech in stories.
5 Look at the work of good writers and see how they do it.

Read this article carefully and then:

1 Work out where the paragraph breaks should come.
2 Explain in a few words what each paragraph is about.

Anaheim, Disneyland and around

In the early 1950s, Walt Disney conceived a theme park where his already hugely popular cartoon characters - Micky Mouse, Donald Duck and the rest - could come to life, to enchant children and make their Uncle Walt even richer. Anaheim was chosen as the location for Disneyland on the basis that these acres of orange groves, thirty miles southeast of downtown, would become LA's next focus of population growth - which indeed they did. The whole area is now overrun with hotels and restaurants (when Disney opened his next theme park, in Florida, he made sure he owned all of them too, thus retaining total corporate control), and the boom doesn't look like slowing. If you're not coming to see Disneyland, you may as well give the place a miss: it hasn't an ounce of interest in itself. To make the most of Disneyland - the ultimate escapist fantasy and the blueprint for imitations worldwide - throw yourself right into it. Don't think twice about anything and go on every ride you can. The high admission price (£25) includes them all, although during peak periods each one can entail hours of queueing. Remember, too, that the emphasis is on family fun; the authorities take a dim view of anything remotely anti-social and eject those that they consider guilty. Over four hundred 'imaginers' worked to create the Indiana Jones Adventure, Disneyland's biggest opening in years. Two hours of queueing are built into the ride, with an interactive archaeological dig and 1930s-style newsreel show leading up to the main feature - a giddy journey along 2500ft of skull-encrusted corridors in which you face fireballs, falling rubble, venomous snakes and, inevitably, a rolling boulder finale. Among the best of the older rides are two in Adventureland: the Pirates of the Caribbean, a boat trip through underground caverns, singing along with drunken pirates; and the Haunted Mansion, a riotous 'doom buggy' tour in the company of the house spooks. Tomorrowland is Disney's vision of the future, where the Space Mountain roller-coaster zips through the pitch-blackness of outer space, and Michael Jackson dances in 3-D. The Skyway cable cars that connect it with the clever but cloyingly sentimental Fantasyland are the only spot in the park from which you can see the outside world. As for accommodation, try to visit Disneyland just for the day and spend the night somewhere else. Most of the hotels and motels nearby cost well in excess of £50 per night. You're not permitted to bring your own food to the park; you can only consume fast food produced on the premises. Disneyland is at 1313 Harbor Blvd, Anaheim, 45 minutes by car from downtown using the Santa Ana Freeway. In summer, the park is open daily between 8am and 1am; otherwise opening hours are weekdays 10am to 6pm, Saturday 9am to midnight, and Sunday 9am to 10pm.

Check: *Now check your answers on page 147.*

Writing practice

You now have an opportunity to practise a number of the skills you have been studying in this chapter. On the next page there is a GCSE exam answer. It needs careful re-thinking and re-writing. Re-write it:

- using the same ideas and approach
- correcting the grammar
- correcting mistakes in spelling and punctuation
- adding material to liven it up, where it is weak and unimaginative.

A tipycal ~~se~~ scene in a supermarket ~~is~~ on a Saturday morning is awful as their is a lot of people shopper as they couldn't last week because they were working.

When you first walk in to a supermarket you ~~ort~~ automatically get a trolley and start to shop. After a while you either forget what your want or they just have not could what you need.

Your in the supermarket for ages because you crushed together like a sandwich. you can't get out. But after a while you manage to wriggle out and go and get more ~~supples~~ supplys and ~~is~~ then ~~on~~ the ~~queae~~ que for ages as their is only one person on the tills

When you do get served and packed all your food, vegatables, etc you just want to go home and relax. But you can't as you have to ~~up~~ unpack the shopping and make it neat within the cupboards, and then you can sit down with a cup of tea and relax to watch the ~~tv~~ television.

4 Punctuation

Punctuation is essential to make written English readable. Poor punctuation is almost always a sign of a weak examination answer. Look at this short extract from a description of a stage performance:

> Everyone became disappointed but all of a sudden a person appeared on the stage.
> It was the 'King of Rock and Roll' Elvis Presley himself, everyone in the crowd looked stunned with amazement. An individual shouted the king is back from the dead.

Nine punctuation mistakes in only 43 words! This is what it should be:

> Everyone became disappointed, but all of a sudden a person appeared on the stage: it was the 'King of Rock and Roll', Elvis Presley himself. Everyone in the crowd looked stunned with amazement. An individual shouted, 'The king is back from the dead!'

This chapter will help you learn how to make punctuation work for you. It explains:

- what each punctuation mark means, and how it should be used
- how to use punctuation to achieve the effects you want.

Contents

Introduction 60
Punctuation marks
Full stop 62
Question mark 62
Exclamation mark 63
Capital letter 64
Apostrophe 66
Quotation marks 66
Comma 68
Colon 70
Semicolon 70
Dash 72
Hyphen 72
Brackets 72
Using punctuation
Paragraphing 74
Abbreviation 76
Direct speech 77
Drama script 79
Putting things in brackets 81
General practice 82
You can get it right! 87

Introduction

If the punctuation is not there to guide your readers, they have to work a lot harder to understand what you mean. Look at the following three examples of badly punctuated writing. They are all taken from students' GCSE coursework entries.

Extract 1

This extract is taken from an account of how burglars get into people's homes:

The Main Ways they do this is by looking out in a street during day and night Without being Suspected for example they Would See if the house is left iN the dark overNight, Knock on doors pretending to be from the Council or a Salesman and if No-one is home theN this is his Next target also if there is SomeonNe iN he Will try to make his Way into your home preteNding to be the gas man or from the Council then he/She Would try to get you out of the room for a few minutes theN he would fill his bag With goodies theN finish his Visit.

Comment

Capital letters should only be used to show such things as:

- the beginning of a sentence
- the first letter of proper nouns
- parts of the name of something, or a title.

This piece could make readers feel confused - even if they made it to the end of such a long sentence without running out of breath.

Extract 2

This is taken from a letter about how footballers should behave:

.... the footballers are supposed to act in a better way than some of the fans who often start fighting on the terraces and children think of Cantona as a hero and they might start copying him.

Comment

When you first read this it sounds as though the fans are fighting on the children, as well as on the terraces! To make better sense there need to be two sentences:

The footballers are supposed to act in a better way than some of the fans who often start fighting on the terraces. Children think of Cantona as a hero and they might start copying him.

(Of course, you might also want to try to re-write the first sentence to improve the flow.)

Extract 3

This is taken from an essay describing a character in a novel:

Mr. Gryce which is the headmaster is not very nice to Billy we can see this on page 54 where Gryce states that he's not happy with Billy 'fast asleep during the lords prayer! I'll thrash you, you irreverent scoundrel I think most of the time he's Just looking for an excuse to tell Somebody off.

Comment

The student has not closed the quotation marks, so the reader could be forgiven for thinking that all of the text to the end of the sentence is what Mr Gryce says to Billy. In which case, the text does not make sense.

Good punctuation = better marks

When you look at passages like these, it is easy to see why poor punctuation costs students marks in exams and coursework.

You may have realised that if you leave out punctuation you lose marks, but did you also know that *you can lose marks if you put punctuation in the wrong place*?

It is important to make sure that your punctuation sends the right message to the reader. Look at these examples and the comments and questions about them:

Louise kissed Darren and his mate, Sean began to laugh.

It seems that Louise is kissing two lads. How can you change the punctuation to make it clear that Louise kissed only Darren?

Nassim knew all his brother's friends. Salima knew all her sisters' friends.

How many brothers has Nassim? Has Salima one sister or more than one? What makes you think this?

How can you avoid confusing your readers and losing marks?

The simple answer is that you need to decide to learn how to use punctuation correctly, and work at breaking any bad writing habits.

This is not as difficult as it seems – the rest of the chapter shows you how punctuation works and gives you opportunities to practise and improve. The hard part is being determined to change, and only **you** can do that.

Full stop

You use a full stop to show your readers that:

1 **They have come to the end of a sentence:**
The jar was empty.

2 **The word you have written is an abbreviation.**
When some words are shortened a full stop is needed at the end of the abbreviation:
Oct. is the abbreviation of *October*.

See page 76 for more on **abbreviations.**

3 **The letters you have written are initials.**
This means they stand for a name or a word. You need to put a full stop after each initial:
S.A.E. for *stamped addressed envelope* or *U.K.* for *United Kingdom*.

Ellipsis

Ellipsis is written as three full stops in a row. It is used:

1 **To show you have left out part of a quotation:**
'A stitch in time...'
The rest of the proverb ('*...saves nine.*') should be where the three full stops are.
'A rose by any other...sweet.'
The middle of the quotation (*...name would smell as...*) has been omitted.

2 **To show someone is hesitating while they speak:**
'No...er, I mean yes.'
The three full stops show where the speaker paused.

3 **To show when a speaker trails off without finishing a sentence:**
'I'll show you...' she finished lamely.

Question mark

1 **Use a question mark to show that a direct question is being asked:**
'Where is Peter today?'

2 **It can also be used, especially in direct speech, to turn a statement into a question:**
'You really mean that?' he said.

Note: If the question is not actually being asked but is just being reported, you do not need a question mark. This is called an indirect question.
She asked him if he wanted to go ice-skating with her.

Exclamation mark

Use exclamation marks to show someone is expressing a strong emotion such as anger: *How dare you!* or delight: *Excellent!*

The following extracts are from three students' GCSE coursework about the lottery. Which student needs to improve their use of each of these punctuation marks:

(a) full stops
(b) question marks
(c) exclamation marks?

Re-write these extracts with the correct punctuation.

A The lottery makes life enjoyable, what is wrong with that

B It gives people the chance to dream about being multi-millionaires. As for the prize money being too large, get serious who wouldn't be happy if they won so much? I would.

C I am writing to you because of what the reverend said and I think that what he said is rubbish because if you win the lottery Jackpot you don't have to work ever again your children won't have to work and if your family need help or friends financially wise you can sort it out for them.

Check: *Now check your answers on page 148.*

Writing practice

Re-write this piece of coursework making sure that your new version is written in sentences.

The main ways they do this is by looking out in a street during day and night without being suspected for example they would see if the house is left in the dark overnight, knock on doors pretending to be from the council or a salesman and if no one is in he will try to make his way into your home pretending to be the gas man or from the council, then he/she would fill his bag with goodies then finish his visit.

Capital letter

Even if you think you know all the rules about using capital letters you still need to read this page carefully. The last rule in particular is a little tricky and one which many people get wrong.

1 **Begin a sentence with a capital letter:**
The door slammed shut.

2 **The personal pronoun 'I' must be written as a capital letter:**
Then I ran away.
It is easy to check that you have got this rule right, because the word 'I' on its own always has to be a capital.

3 **Initials must be capitals:**
S.E. Hinton, N.S.P.C.C.

4 **Acronyms should be in capitals.** (Acronyms are words formed from the initial letters of other words.)
ASH, NATO

5 **After opening quotation marks, use a capital letter for the start of the speech.**

See page 77 for more on **direct speech.**

6 **Begin a proper name with a capital letter.**
A proper name means it is unique. For example:
- *there are lots of men but only one* Michael Douglas
- *there are lots of days but only one that is* Christmas Day
- *there are lots of princes but only one* Prince William
- *and there are lots of books but only one called* Buddy.

However, not all the words in long proper names or titles of books, plays, songs, and articles begin with a capital letter. For titles and any proper names made up of more than three words, all the words should begin with capitals except:
- *a, an, the*
- two or three letter prepositions such as: *of, by, in*
- conjunctions such as: *of, by, in, to, and, or, but.*
But if one of these words is the first or last word of a proper name or title, it should begin with a capital as well.

Still confused? Look at these examples to help you:
Department of Education and Employment
'As Time Goes By' *'North by Northwest'*
'Of Mice and Men' *'Lord of the Flies'*

SELF TEST

1 Read this paragraph from a student's essay which describes the two main characters, Anne and Loomis, from the book *Z For Zachariah*. Then make separate lists of:

- all the words in which capital letters are wrongly used
- any words which the writer forgot to give capital letters.

She AlwayS seemed to be occupied with things to do. She didn't have a big Family She Just lived with her mum and dad and her little brother they also Owned a farm. on Loomis's Side he was a Scientist Who worked on Special plastics (he made the Safe Suit this way). he would have Probably been in his laboratory for Most OF his time working.

2 Write out the story below, putting in the missing capital letters. Check your answers at the end of each section.

(a) *in the distance i could see that darren had already started the ford fiesta and was pulling away from the southgate test centre.*

(b) *suddenly i realised there was a problem: mr steep, his instructor, had already got out of the car, but the examiner, mr acton, had not yet got in. realising what had happened, mother began to run after the car as darren gathered speed and turned the corner into bell street.*

(c) *both darren, mother and the fiesta disappeared from view. there was a sudden squeal of brakes, a scream of, 'no!' from my mother and a loud crash.*

(d) *this would make a good entry for the book 'how to fail your driving test' by ivor smash, i decided.*

(e) *since darren had run over a fox and hit a lamp post, we had to call out both the rspca and the aa. when dad and i asked him about it, all darren could say was, 'perhaps i need a new pair of glasses.'*

3 Using the rules on the previous page to help you, look through two pieces of your written work. Which mistakes do you make?

Check: *The answers to questions 1 and 2 are on page 149.*

Apostrophe

Some people use so many apostrophes that their work looks as if it has measles; other people do not use any. It is easy to get it right once you know the rules. There are only two reasons for using an apostrophe:

1 **When letters have been left out.**
The apostrophe shows where the letter or letters were taken out: *didn't* (did not), *we'll* (we will), *can't* (cannot).

2 **To show ownership.**
When you are writing, ask yourself how many 'owners' there are. Then:
- If there is only one owner, just add ***apostrophe*** and ***-s***:
the bone belonging to the dog – the dog's bone
the Eve of New Year – New Year's Eve.
- If there is more than one owner, look at the plural word being used:
  - if the plural ends in ***-s***, just add an apostrophe:
  the medals of the Olympic swimmers – the Olympic swimmers' medals
  - if the plural does not end in ***s***, add ***apostrophe*** and ***-s***:
  the Christmas party for the children – the children's Christmas party.

Exception: *its = of it, it's = it is*
It's a pity the cat caught its paw in the cat flap.

Quotation marks

Quotation marks (inverted commas) are easy to use as long as you remember to open and close them. They are used to mark the beginning and end of:

1 **Direct speech**, where words are actually spoken by a character:
'Are you going to the party on Saturday?' asked Matthew.

2 **Quotations:**
'More haste less speed.'

3 **Titles of works** such as magazines, newspapers, articles or short stories, poems, songs, and radio or television programmes:
'Star Trek'

Single quotation marks are normally used, but if you need to write a second set of quotation marks inside direct speech or a quotation, use double quotation marks:
'Did you watch "Casualty" on Saturday?' she asked.

SELF TEST

1 Look carefully at these examples of students' coursework. Work out which words need to have apostrophes added, and which need to have them taken out. Then re-write the sentences correctly.

(a) *Boxer became faithful to the pigs because he could not think thing's out for himself, so he accepted the pigs as his teacher's and believed everything that was told to him.*

(b) *Well its up to you to make your choice but always do your best and you will succeed.*

(c) *Im' writing to you in concern about an article I read in a magazine.*

2 Work out whether quotation marks have been used correctly here. Then re-write the sentences correctly.

(a) *An individual shouted the King is back from the dead.*

(b) *The two films are based on the same thing, nuclear war, but they are very different. When the wind Blows is a cartoon and Threads is a drama documentary.*

(c) *The supermarket aisle was filled with potatoes, fresh carrots and cauliflowers and a wonderfully 'earthy' smell, I would have preferred the ... meat section. Here the carnivores were readily buying the 'half price beef' that was on offer.*

3 Darren Franks is good at explaining what job he does, but this article needs to have its apostrophes replaced as you re-write it. Darren, an apprentice chef at The Landmark Hotel, London, said:

'First off, Im a chef, not a cook. I get wound up by that mistake. I dont like the word 'cook' – Im more of an artiste than that.

I left school after doing work experience here one summer, and Ive been an apprentice for eight months. Hopefully, Ill end up as a celebrity chef with my own restaurant like Marco Pierre-White.

Nobodys ever called me a girl. In fact people are quite impressed because my jobs unusual.'

Check: *Now check your answers on page 149.*

Comma

There are a number of reasons for commas to be used. These can be divided into four main groups:

1 **A comma is a signal that the reader needs to pause:**

- so that the sentence will not be misunderstood:
  As the hero ran in the audience began to applaud.

  A comma is needed to stop it sounding as if the hero is running into the audience. It should read:
  As the hero ran in, the audience began to applaud.
- when quotation marks are opened in mid-sentence:
  Simone muttered, 'I didn't break it.'

See page 77 for more about **direct speech.**

2 **Commas are used to separate sections of a sentence:**

- The items in a list:
  He ordered a cola, some fries, a beefburger, and ice cream.
  Some people say you do not need a comma before *and*, but sentences like this one could be confusing if you missed it out: *beefburger and ice-cream*? So it's best to play safe and put it in.
- Sometimes a sentence contains a section that could be left out and the sentence would still make sense:
  My Aunt Doris, who used to live in Dorking, has a pet chimpanzee.
  The words *who used to live in Dorking*, which are separated by commas, could be left out. It is as if they are 'in brackets':
  My Aunt Doris has a pet chimpanzee.

See page 81 for more about **putting things in brackets.**

3 **Commas can also be used when writing addresses:**
13, Giggs Hill Drive, Thames Ditton, Surrey.
These commas are often left out. The rule is that you should either use them all the time in addresses, or leave them out all the time.

4 **Commas can be used before joining two sentences with a conjunction**, if you think it will make the meaning clearer:
The aerial had snapped off, but they could still tune in to Radio 1.

SELF TEST

1 Explain what is wrong with each of these examples taken from students' coursework.

(a) He said they treated him like dirt. He said 'I can get a job easily, I can be a barman.' I laughed and went home.

(b) The Editor,
Daily Mail
London,

(c) *While packing up Julia found her long lost silver ring.*

2 Copy these sentences adding commas so that they make sense.

(a) *American football which is played on a pitch marked with parallel lines is sometimes known as 'gridiron football'.*

(b) *Similar to the game of rugby American football is a contact sport.*

(c) *An oval ball and rugby-like goal posts are used but, unlike rugby players have to be well-padded and wear helmets.*

(d) *Only eleven players although there are many more in a team are allowed on the pitch at any one time.*

(e) *A game has four quarters and a quarter lasts fifteen minutes.*

3 Copy out these sentences adding, moving or removing commas so that they make sense.

(a) *Though, Andy kept on, watching the football tackles alarmed him.*

(b) *The referee blew his whistle at Paul, and his team mates, began to jeer.*

(c) *The policewoman who was carrying, Cantona's shoe jumped onto the horse.*

(d) *The bill, had to be paid but the team's manager, had disappeared.*

(e) *Since there was no one else, around the goalkeeper tried on the thin captain's suit.*

4 Which mistakes do you tend to make with commas? Look through two pieces of your coursework and use the rules on the facing page to help you improve.

Check: *Now check your answers to questions 1–3 on page 150.*

Colon

A colon is needed to introduce such things as:

1 **A list:**
The drawer contained: pencils, pens, rulers, compasses, protractor, and calculators.

2 **An explanation or an example:**
Camouflage is vitally important to many animals: it allows them to blend in with their surroundings to avoid being detected by other animals.

3 **The words spoken in a drama script:**
RAJA: *Where did you put my coat?*

4 **A long speech or quotation (instead of a comma):**
The headteacher addressed the whole school: 'What I have to say to you is very serious.'

Semicolon

Often it is a matter of personal style whether you should use a semicolon rather than another piece of punctuation. However, once you have learned how to use a semicolon, you will find it is a useful tool.
Semicolons have two main uses:

1 **They can join two or more sentences which are linked in subject matter to form one sentence:**
Many of the local factories had shut; it was harder to find work.
When you use a semicolon in this way conjunctions such as *and* and *but* are not needed.

2 **They can separate items in a list when you need to use punctuation within the phrases in your list:**
You can take care of your health by: giving up smoking, which is linked to heart disease, lung cancer and bronchitis; taking exercise; reducing your intake of alcohol to 21 units a week for men, 14 for women; eating a varied diet containing plenty of fresh fruit and vegetables, protein, carbohydrates, and polyunsaturated fats rather than saturated fats; and not becoming obese.

1 Copy these sentences, adding a colon where necessary.

(a) *Contestants win one of these prizes a holiday, a television, a car or a cuddly toy.*

(b) *The rules in this game are simple the first one to answer wins the point.*

2 Decide how the students, whose work appears below, could have improved their coursework by making use of colons.

(a)

> And finally the shop manager. A breed that evolved through managing to do as little work as possible and looking extremely similar to a Butlin's red coat.

(b)

> *a few days after I moved in we were brought together and introduced as 'Annie, your friend' and 'Jo, your new friend' respectively.*

3 Pair up the following sentences so that each pair can be linked using a semicolon. Then copy out the new, longer sentences making sure you punctuate them correctly.

(i) When his luck ran out and he had gambled his last penny, he played the guitar and begged.

(ii) The Minister said that the parents must sign the contracts too.

(iii) The holiday brochure promised a mesmerising view from the roof garden.

(iv) The cost of rugby shirts has increased once again.

(v) It was getting late: the wedding guests had got lost.

(a) Perhaps a sponsor can be persuaded to donate some extra funds.

(b) If only they had been given a map, rather than being told to follow James.

(c) When things went better and he won, he would stay in a room at the Ritz.

(d) If any of them refused, then it would only make the situation worse.

(e) Two pots of peonies and a glimpse of the local bus station weren't quite what she had expected.

Check: *Now check your answers on page 150.*

Dash

Dashes can be used in pairs or singly. The main thing to remember is to use dashes sparingly - if they are over-used they lose their impact. You can use them:

1 **As a pair**. Dashes can separate a group of words within a sentence in the same way as pairs of commas or brackets:
Ben - now without a friend in the world - was very jealous.

2 **Singly.** A single dash can be used before an explanation or example. This is less formal than a colon:
None of the videos was high quality - they had all been pirated.
Using a dash near the end of a sentence is a way of showing a sharp change in thought. Usually the sentence moves to a surprising ending:
Michael found himself praying that a bolt of lightning would strike Mr Jones the games teacher - even a small one would do.

Hyphen

There are three reasons for using a hyphen:

1 **To join the two parts of a compound word.** (A compound word is made by joining two other words.)
dry-clean, heart-breaking, cold-shoulder, double-park
This can be confusing because sometimes the same word is written in different ways. For example, all of these are correct:
paper knife, paper-knife, paperknife

2 **To show that certain describing words belong together:**
On show at the museum were the skeletons of long-dead animals.
Without the hyphen it would suggest that the dead animals had long bodies!

3 **If you come to the end of a line and can only fit in part of the word you are writing, then it is possible to use a hyphen.** This shows that the rest of the word will follow. Since you can only break a word at the end of a syllable, save yourself time and effort by writing the whole word on a new line. As far as possible, when handwriting, you should avoid hyphenating words at the ends of lines.

Brackets

See page 81 for more on **putting things in brackets.**

You can use a pair of brackets to enclose information in the sentence that is not strictly needed, but tells you something of interest. Without the brackets the sentence would sound rather muddled:

Cyril Falkerson (named after his father) had climbed Everest.

SELF TEST

1 Study these examples of students' GCSE work and suggest ways they could be improved using dashes, and brackets.

(a) *But he clearly loves dogs, that or he has them for protection.*

(b) As you are crossing keep looking. And don't run, you could fall over. But don't walk slower than a snail, you will want to get across the road before the next car comes speeding along.

2 Copy out these sentences adding dashes to make the meaning clearer.

(a) *Marie who hated all reptiles was longing to go back to the hotel.*

(b) *'For years tourists were not allowed to visit turtle beaches after dark their torches might mislead the turtles,' explained the guide.*

(c) *Hearing a turtle lumbering towards her, Marie switched on her light it wasn't every day she had the chance to confuse a tortoise.*

(d) *The turtles were plodding a long way up the beaches they needed to lay their eggs above the high tide mark.*

(e) *Some day the baby turtles would hatch no doubt looking like miniature prehistoric monsters.*

3 Re-write this advertisement for hair shampoo by adding:

- hyphens in the first sentence
- dashes in the rest of the paragraph.

Having problems finding some get up and go in the mornings? New 'Lemon and Mint' shampoo and conditioner for oily hair from Original Mint Source have the most invigorating fragrance we've ever tried guaranteed to wake up the laziest of sleepyheads.

Check: *Now check your answers on page 151.*

Using punctuation

Paragraphing

Breaking your work up into paragraphs is an important way to make it easy to follow. The break between paragraphs allows readers to pause and take in your train of thought. You can help your readers in the following ways:

See pages 53–55 for more on **paragraphs.**

1 Make it clear you have begun a new paragraph by writing the first word about two centimetres in from the margin. This is called 'indenting'.

2 Start a new paragraph every time you change what you are writing about. This means that when you write about a new:

- time
- place
- person
- action
- idea

you should begin a new paragraph.

SELF TEST

In this letter about the evils of the trade in mahogany, each sentence forms a separate paragraph, making the letter seem very bitty. Which sentences could you link into paragraphs?

1 The article was showing the plight of the Indians living in the Amazon.

2 I was deeply shocked by the information it gave and feel as though I should do something to help.

3 The Indians are being pursued by Brazilian timber cutters to let them cut down the rain forest for the mahogany trade.

4 These forests are the Indian's lifeline and taking it away means death for the Indians.

5 If the Indians refuse, after seeing through the deception and greed of the 'timber cutters' who by now will have tried everything from bribery to threatening behaviour, then their lives become under threat from these dangerous people.

6 There are accounts of these 'timber cutters' opening fire on tribes of helpless Indians, killing women and children too.

Check: *Now check your answers on page 151.*

SELF TEST

The following is a newspaper article relating the true story of how Ann Brewer hatched eleven quails from some eggs she bought in her local supermarket.

This version of the article has no paragraphs. As you can see, the text does not look very appealing to a reader if it is not broken up.
Re-write the story in paragraphs and indent each one.

Note: there were 10 paragraphs in the original version.

DINNER HATCHED

Wife raises 11 quail chicks from supermarket eggs

Quail eggs seemed the ideal exotic starter for Ann Brewer's dinner party. Three weeks later, she gave her friends even more to talk about by hatching chicks from three of them. Mrs Brewer took the eggs off the menu after accidentally breaking one and finding it to be fertile. So she put the remaining 11 in an incubator and chose melon as a substitute first course. Now she has hatched eight more quail chicks after buying a further two dozen brown speckled eggs from her local branch of Waitrose. Mrs Brewer, a 59-year-old poultry breeder, explained: 'It was a case of placing them under a lamp in the warm and waiting to see what happened. 'As long as the eggs are fertile and the yolks haven't been broken then they should hatch.' Mrs Brewer, who also runs kennels with her husband William near Petersfield, Hampshire, said the 11 young birds would be sold to a breeder. Fertilised quail eggs have a small white spot in the yolk. In Britain, quail – a small game bird the size of a pigeon – is regarded as a delicacy. An estimated nine million of its eggs are eaten each year, selling for £1.20 per dozen. Mrs Brewer's eggs were supplied by the FayreGame company. Managing director Nick White said hens were put in to lay at six weeks – an age when it is difficult to identify and exclude male birds. He added: 'I would say that five per cent of quail eggs on the shelves are fertile. They are absolutely harmless.'

***Check:** Now check your answer on page 152.*

Abbreviation

It is not always easy to know how to write an abbreviation, but the safest way is to follow these rules:

1 **If the abbreviation is made up of capital letters which are initials, place a full stop after each initial:**
National Society for the Protection of Children → N.S.P.C.C.

2 **If the abbreviation is an acronym** (a word made up of initials) **full stops are not needed:**
RADAR

3 **When the abbreviation is made from only the first part of the word, it should end with a full stop:**
South Glamorgan → S. Glam.

4 **If the first letter of the word begins the abbreviation and the last letter of the word ends the abbreviation, no full stop is needed:**
Doctor → Dr

If none of these rules seem to apply and you do not know whether to add a full stop or not, **leave the full stop out.**

1 Look at this special offer promising an extra night's free accommodation at a hotel. If you were following formal abbreviation rules, what is wrong with the way it has been punctuated in the brochure?

> **SPECIAL OFFER:** 3rd night free Nov 1 – Dec 24 '96 & '97 and Jan 2 – Mar 20 & Jul/Aug.

2 The following was published as a weather report.

> LONDON & SOUTH EAST: There will be some sunny spells but also showers, heavy at times. Max 8c (46f)

How should it have been written to follow formal abbreviation rules?

Check: *Now check your answers on page 152.*

Direct speech

Many students lose marks in their exam or coursework because they do not punctuate quotations correctly. You need not be one of them if you learn these simple rules:

1 If the speech is introduced by some words, like 'she said', a comma is needed before the quotation marks are opened.

2 The words which are spoken have to be enclosed inside a pair of single quotation marks.

Jan pushed open the bedroom door and stepped into the room. Immediately she was engulfed in darkness and the smell of rotting banana skins.

(a) 'Is there a humanoid life-form in here?' she asked.

Silence.

Striding across to where the window should be, soft lumps of what she hoped were only clothes and rustling packets slithered beneath her feet.

(b) Jan tried again, 'Steven!'

She left a dramatic pause but there was still no answer. Leaning forward Jan felt for and then tugged at a long swathe of fabric.

Light burst into the room.

'Ugh Mum!' came an indignant voice.

(c) 'Ugh Steven!' she responded, 'the estate agent's coming at two o'clock. If you don't want to halve the value of this house, will you please get up and sort this carnage out.'

Steven's face had finally appeared, 'All right, you don't have to nag,' he said, then pulling the black duvet back over his head, 'I'll get up in a minute.'

3 A speech has to begin with a capital letter. Then, the rest of it is punctuated like any other sentence.

4 The speech must have punctuation before the quotation marks close. If a full stop, exclamation mark or question mark is not needed, a comma should be used.

6 Make sure it is clear who is speaking each time.

5 When the next speaker talks, begin a new paragraph.

And finally … look back through the text for each of these features and make sure you have worked out how to write:

- (a) speech which comes at the beginning of a sentence
- (b) speech which comes at the end of a sentence
- (c) speech which is interrupted mid-sentence and then begins again.

SELF TEST

1 Look at these examples taken from students' stories. Can you spot the mistakes they made when writing direct speech? Re-write these conversations so that they are punctuated correctly.

(a)

'What is the matter' Jenny's mum said.
'It's not fair, they keep picking on me' Jenny cried.
'Why, what have they done' replied Mum sympathetically.

(b)

'No, I'd better not because I'm having my dinner soon,.' Said Jeremy.
'Okay then, we'll see you at school on Monday' said Colin.
'Bye'. They all shouted.

2 One of the biggest problems many people have with direct speech is knowing when to put in commas, and when to leave them out. Practise this skill by copying the direct speech below and adding in commas where needed.

(a) *The examiner asked 'Can you explain how factory farming works?'*

(b) *'Poultry or animals are housed in confined spaces' Tara said.*

(c) *Then pointing at the photograph she continued 'They're fed on high protein foods.'*

(d) *'Yes' said the examiner 'and do you know anything else about the feed stuffs?'*

(e) *'No' Tara admitted 'but I know that battery hens lay more eggs than free range chickens.'*

3 Look through some of your own coursework. Which mistakes do you tend to make when you are writing direct speech? Make a list of the rules you need to work at, then learn them.

Check: *Now check your answers to questions 1 and 2 on page 152.*

Drama script

Many students forget that drama scripts do not need speech marks. Look carefully at the example below to see how a drama script should be set out:

1 The name of the character speaking is on the left hand side in the margin. It should be written in capital letters.

2 A colon is needed after the speaker's name and before the speech begins.

JAN: Is there a humanoid life-form in here?

(She walks across to the curtains.)

Steven!

(Jan draws the curtains and light fills the filthy bedroom.)

STEVEN: Ugh Mum!

JAN: Ugh Steven! The estate agent's coming at two o'clock. If you don't want to halve the value of this house, will you please get up and sort this carnage out.

STEVEN: All right, you don't have to nag. I'll get up in a minute.

3 The speech begins with a capital letter and is punctuated like any other sentence, which means that a full stop, question mark or exclamation mark is needed at the end of the speech.

4 Stage directions are enclosed in brackets and underlined.

SELF TEST

1 Both these students made mistakes while writing drama scripts. Can you spot the mistakes and write the scripts correctly?

(a)

Interviewer: *"Hello this is Radio 1!" "Now I'm going to be speaking to a professional arcade machine gambler, who claims to be earning £120 a day from machines."*

Terry: *"Yes, that's right, well, on average."*

(b)

Inter *Hello, Mr Freeman.*

Mr Free *Hello, How are you?*

2 Read this conversation, which is written as indirect speech, then re-write it as a correctly punctuated drama script. Slight variations on the wording of the speech are possible.

Karen told him that the concert tickets cost fifty pounds. Mark explained that he did not have the money on him. Karen asked him to give her the money when he saw her later. Mark said that he would have to borrow some money from his mother. Karen asked if his mother would lend him the money. Mark said he was not sure, but she might. Karen wanted to know how he was going to pay his mother back and Mark explained that he would be starting a Saturday job working in a computer shop next month. Karen said that it was great news that he had got the job. Mark asked if she had had any luck looking for work and Karen explained that she was baby-sitting regularly for Jo, her neighbour, but did not want a Saturday job because she needed the time free to get her schoolwork done.

3 Look through a script you have written. Which mistakes do you tend to make when you write a drama script?

4 Choose four speeches from your script which have mistakes in them. Re-write these, setting them out and punctuating them correctly.

Check: *Now check your answers to questions 1 and 2 on page 153.*

Putting things in brackets

If you want to separate part of a sentence, you can use brackets. However, there are times when you might prefer to use commas or dashes. When you are deciding what to do, follow these two rules:

1 Whichever you use - brackets, commas or dashes - you must remember that they always come in pairs: one at the beginning and one at the end of the words you want to separate from the rest of the sentence.

2 Choosing the best punctuation marks depends on understanding the style of writing being used.
   - Brackets are more serious, so they are used in formal writing such as a literature essay or scientific report.
   - Commas are slightly less formal, and the most commonly used.
   - Dashes are much more relaxed - you might use them in a letter to a friend.

Look at the sentences below and decide whether brackets, commas or dashes would be the best choice for enclosing the parts of the sentence which have been underlined. Write out the sentence as you think it should be punctuated. On a separate line explain the reason for your decision.

1 *A hand written note scribbled in green ink was taped firmly across the letter box.*
2 *The tour of the docks built in 1905 will begin at 2.30 p.m.*
3 *Readers of the 'Daily Herald' will be pleased to know that Lui Chan who once played for Torton Wanderers has offered to coach the team.*
4 *'Well, it was like this: the lads who had come on the trip some of them as young as thirteen had just got a bit bored with waiting ...'*
5 *The court should know that Michael Smith the defendant has up until now always been thought of as one of Lightwater High School's best students.*
6 *Thank you for the beautiful coat. It was just right green has always been my favourite colour and I shall really enjoy wearing it this winter.*

***Check:** Now check your answers on page 153.*

General practice

This section begins with more practice on individual punctuation marks. At the end are several passages from which all the punctuation has been removed. These will help you practise thinking about punctuation while you write.

Capital letter

Copy each section of the story, removing any capital letters which are misplaced. *Check your answers on page 154.*

1 Donna had just filled the front of her Trolley from the Fruit and Vegetable section at Tesco's when she remembered the Magazine for her Mother.
2 Leaving the trolley by the Bananas she went to collect 'Art Of Good Cooking' before continuing with her shopping.
3 Up and down the aisles she steered, remembering the Shredded Wheat, Coca Cola, bread, rice, Custard Powder, and even that they preferred Brazilian coffee beans.
4 In the Household Goods aisle, she noticed a stranger staring into her trolley. Donna headed away from the cans of Mr Sheen polish and towards the check-out.
5 One last treat. She would have a Chocolate Bar. Placing the Crunchie on the conveyor belt Donna began to pile up her shopping behind it.
6 'These aren't mine,' she said, holding up a punnet of Strawberries, 'Nor these!' She had found a bag of pears.
7 'No,' came a Voice from behind her, 'They're mine.'
It was the stranger who had stared at her trolley.
8 'Someone took my trolley from beside the Bananas,' He said. 'It must have been you.'

Full stop

Copy these sentences, removing full stops that are misused and adding in any that are missing. *Check your answers on page 154.*

1 Tom knew this was the dog he wanted. When the Alsatian chewed at his trainers.
2 'Are you sure?.' Sandy was not pleased, 'I don't want our home destroyed .!'

3 'Well he er he's probably just hungry. I'm sure that, once he's fed regularly, he'll stop'
4 ' You should ask the RSPCA officer. Whether this dog will be happy in a small flat.'

Apostrophe

Re-write these sentences, making sure the apostrophe is used correctly. *Check your answers on page 155.*

1 'Theres no way Ill be home by ten,' said Chris.
2 Both the tyres on Chriss bike were completely flat.
3 'Theyv'e been cut - theres' a hole in each of em,' Chris said.
4 'Do'nt worry. Youd better borrow mine. It's over there,' Alex offered.
5 'No, its not,' Chris said. 'It's saddle is, but the rest of its' gone.'

Quotation marks (inverted commas)

Copy the following sentences adding quotation marks (also known as inverted commas) where necessary. *Check your answers on page 155.*

1 Do you keep back copies of The Times? he asked the librarian.
2 No, he said, but we do have CD-Roms of The Times and The Guardian.
3 Good, I'm looking for an article about an episode of Panorama. I think it was called Watching the Detectives, he explained.
4 I remember that, he said, wasn't it about video camera surveillance?

General test A

The article below is divided into paragraphs but the rest of the punctuation has been removed. Re-write the passage, putting in all the necessary punctuation so that it reads clearly. *Check your answers on page 155.*

Hermie the hamster demolished our pub

i only paid £3 for hermie my pet hamster but hes ended up costing almost £1000

it all started one friday evening at our hotel pub in the isle of man id just taken hermie out of his cage when my dog sue a bull mastiff ran into my bedroom and knocked us both flying

5 hermie was so scared he hid in a tiny hole in the skirting and wouldnt budge i tried to put my hand in to get him out but the hole was too small

dad said hermie would come out when he was ready but i was worried hed starve to death so i persuaded dad to remove the floorboards he and my uncle couldnt remove them completely cause of my fitted wardrobes but they wedged a few

10 open

there was no sign of hermie in the morning and after wed waited all afternoon to no avail dad started nailing down the floorboards

suddenly dad accidentally hit a hot water pipe by the time a plumber arrived my bed was soaking and water was seeping into the pub below then the plumber

15 scratched my wardrobes ripping up the boards i thought dad would flip when he had to replaster the bar ceiling but he was really understanding

then on sunday evening dad heard a scratching from behind a wall he was sure it was hermie but there was a radiator in the way dad didnt want to raise my hopes so while i was at school he secretly arranged to rescue him

20 he cut a huge hole above the radiator but when he looked in hermie was too far to reach then mum squeezed his water bottle down the gap and when he crawled up to have a drink she grabbed him

he was skinny and dirty and his little paws were bleeding but at least he was alive the repair bill came to around £1000 and we thought hamsters were cheap pets

General test B

The story below is divided into paragraphs but the rest of the punctuation has been removed. Re-write each paragraph so that it is punctuated correctly. *Check your answers on page 156.*

FASHION VICTIMS

An argument in favour of school uniform?

a young inner city family from london stayed with us the other day
and it is clear that in the past year or so the designer fashion craze
has become an epidemic

not only do the young and even the very young demand the latest
5 in designer wear calvin klein ralph lauren armani timberland
versace moschino carhart tommy hilfiger and so on they hardly now
dare venture on the street unless they have it they were once judged
by the brand name on their trainers they are now judged according
to the label attached to their polo shirts, designer jeans and jackets
10 and copies which abound are spotted immediately they may be
almost identical to the real thing but they dont bear the all
important serial number only the genuine best is acceptable if you
are to have any street credibility even the sunglasses have to come
from aspreys

15 our friend the young mother who had three children displayed
genuine alarm fear even at the extent of the problem
she said you look at the kids hanging about a tenement block in a
very poor area some of them as young as 10 and you have to ask
yourself how can they afford those clothes some of them are
20 wearing £400 or £500 worth the answer is they cant afford it they
have to steal for what they are wearing or parents have to even the
babies wear chipie designer stuff worth £200

the truth is that whereas the outside world links young crime in the
inner cities with drugs it is as often as not associated with the sort of
25 clothes seen in bond street says our friend often the kids have the
stuff torn off them and are left naked its terrifying

**would making pupils wear a strictly enforced school uniform take
some of the pressure off parents and children might it reduce the
number of youth crimes what do you think**

General test C

The passage below is taken from an article which appeared in 'The Times'. All of the punctuation has been removed this time, including paragraphs. Re-write it, putting in all the punctuation it needs for the passage to make good sense. *Check your answers on page 156.*

Note: Start by reading the piece through first so that you have some idea of where new paragraphs will be needed before you start writing.

The Model Railway Passenger

silent rail passengers who never complain about delays ask the way to the buffet or try to strike up conversation are to make an appearance on a seaside branch line the passengers life sized papier mache dummies are to be placed on trains between hull and bridlington as part of a community arts project others will stand or sit at station platforms the dummies will ride on the trains from the end of next month some will be dressed in period costumes of the yorkshire working families who came to bridlington for their holidays earlier this century they will be made in a disused parcel office at bridlington station passengers tourists and local people will be encouraged to help construct them shirley hester of the mental health charity mind which is involved with the project said we hope that people living all along the line will come to help us with the sculptures and even people on holiday for a few days who would like to try their hand at making an arm or a foot we hope it will liven up the station and add to the interest of the journey ken bray a spokesman for regional railways north east said the models will always be accompanied by one or two fare paying adults

You can get it right!

If you want your work to score the best marks, and be easily understood, then bear these points in mind:

1 Punctuation is needed to help readers understand what you have written. If you leave out punctuation marks you can confuse people. Examiners hate being confused – they take off marks for it.

2 Every sentence must begin with a capital letter and end with a full stop. Make sure you know where your sentence is going to end before you start writing it. Too many people lose marks because their sentences ramble on and on and on and ...

3 Most punctuation marks are quite straightforward to use. It is a matter of learning the rules and then making sure that you follow them while you are writing.

4 There are simple rules on how to use each of these:
- paragraphs
- question marks
- exclamation marks
- apostrophes
- colons
- hyphens
- quotation marks

so learn them carefully, and think about them as you write.

5 Other punctuation marks and situations may seem harder to work out, but keep practising. You can learn how to get it right!

6 Focus on improving your use of one punctuation mark at a time. Use this book to help you.

7 Be aware of how punctuation is used in the books you read. Make a habit of looking out for the punctuation mark you are working on. Notice how it is used by good writers and follow their example.

8 Know which mistakes you 'always' make. Then break the habit.

9 Check each piece of writing before handing it in (not just those written in English lessons) and correct any mistakes you spot.

Words and spelling

When you write an exam answer your writing is judged partly by your vocabulary - the words you use - and by how well you can spell them. This chapter is about how to improve both your vocabulary and your spelling.

Contents

How big is your vocabulary?	89	Spelling	100
Vocabulary: get active!	90	Why do people make mistakes?	102
Practice and confidence	91	Spelling survival programme	103
Choosing the right word	92	Spelling rules	104
Parts of a word	94	Seeing double	108
Suffixes	95	Tricky customers	109
Prefixes	96	Words commonly confused	111
Word families	98		

How big is your vocabulary?

Examiners often comment on a student's vocabulary. If the writing is weak they may say it is because the writer has a 'limited vocabulary'. It's not always easy for students to understand either what this means, or what they can do about it.

How does it show?

There are two obvious ways in which limitations in vocabulary show:

- using the wrong word
- repetition of a word when it would be better to use a different word or to express the meaning in a different way.

Of these, repetition is more common; the writer is stuck for a different word and so goes on using the same word over and over again:

> Comparing 'Threads' to 'When the Wind Blows'
>
> The cartoon shows you Jim collecting all the equipment and most of the film is about him building up the refuge.
>
> 'Threads' shows the build up much better than 'When the Wind Blows' by showing newsflashes on the war and it shows it on TV, Radio and in newspapers. It also shows you the people not taking much notice at first

This writer either does not know another word for 'show' or cannot be bothered to stop and find an alternative. If you look the word up in a thesaurus you find:

demonstrate, display, exhibit, disclose, expose, point out, reveal, explain, depict, describe, illustrate

and there are other words, too.

We might re-write the text like this:

> <u>Comparing 'Threads' to 'When the Wind Blows'</u>
>
> The cartoon <u>displays</u> Jim collecting all the equipment and most of the film is about him building up the refuge.
>
> 'Threads' <u>illustrates</u> the build up much better than 'When the Wind Blows' by showing newsflashes on the war and it <u>uses</u> extracts from TV, Radio and in newspapers. It also <u>depicts</u> the people not taking much

It's a fairly safe bet that the writer of the original text knew at least *some* of the words that have been used in this revision.

Vocabulary: get active!

The number of words that you know is described as your **vocabulary**. People who write about language say that we have two vocabularies:

- **our *active* vocabulary**
  words that we can and do use in speaking and writing
- **our *passive* vocabulary**
  words that we recognise when we are reading but which – for some reason – we don't use when writing or speaking.

Group the words below into three lists:

A Words that you know and would feel completely confident about using in a written sentence.
B Words that you recognise and think you know the meaning of, but would probably not use yourself.
C Words that you do not recognise.

multitude	municipal	murmur	mutiny	mutual	myriad
mumble	munificent	muscle	mutt	muzzle	mystery
mummify	mural	muse	mutter	muzzy	mystical
munch	murky	museum	mutton	myopia	myth

You may well find that list **A**, which contains the words in your active vocabulary, is shorter than list **B**, the words in your passive vocabulary.

Practice and confidence

So the question is: how do we get the knowledge and confidence to start using all these 'passive' words so that we can make them 'active'?

1 **Try them out.**
We are often too afraid of making mistakes and being laughed at, so we play safe. On the whole, teachers do not laugh at people who try a new word, so pluck up courage and have a go.

2 **Use word books.**
Make sure that you have a good dictionary and use it regularly. Get access to a thesaurus and make sure that you know how to use it.

3 **Take an interest and be inquisitive.**
When reading, don't let your eye glide over words you don't know:
- try to puzzle out the meaning from the rest of the sentence
- then look the word up in the dictionary to see if you were right.

4 **Try out new words in your head.**
When you encounter new words, don't just make sure you know what they mean; try them out in sentences of your own - in your head. This helps to fit them into your active vocabulary.

SELF TEST

One of the ways we learn new words is when we come across them while reading. Often we work out what they mean from the context, from the sentence they are in. In these sentences there are a number of words underlined. Try to work out what each of them means from the context.

A typical peasant's house at this time had a small garden or yard attached to it. Within this curtilage you might find a cowshed containing the usual fittings and equipment – for example the cogue into which the cow was milked. In the house there would probably be a traditional cradle, also made of wood and lined with something soft, probably bocasin and, in the kitchen, almost certainly a quern. People here made their own bread and the nearest mill was probably far away. So if you grew corn, you had to grind it yourself. The wealthier peasants might have a simple musical instrument with which to provide entertainment in the evenings. There is even a record of one family who owned a mandola – although what this exotic instrument was doing so far away from its native Italy who can tell?

***Check:** Now check your answers on page 157.*

Choosing the right word

The other problem students often have with vocabulary is that they choose the wrong word. Sometimes this is because they know two words that are very similar and pick the wrong one:

> Frank also takes the opportunity to invite Rita to a dinner party which she reluctantly excepts.

The writer should have written *accepts* - a common mistake. There is a list of words which are often confused on page 114.

Unsuitable language

Another mistake students sometimes make is to use a word that is unsuitable for the subject they are writing about or the audience they are writing for. In this example, the student is writing a letter to her M.P. to protest about the felling of tropical hardwood trees in Brazil:

> Dear Sir/Madam
>
> I am writing to express to you my interest and disgust of the mahogany trade. I am not sure if you yourself are aware of the tremendous problem that this trade is causing to Brazilian land and its inhabitants and so hope this letter will educate and enable you to activate against it.

There are several words in this opening paragraph that are not suitable for a letter to an M.P. In the first sentence, the words *interest* and *disgust* sound odd together - *interest* is too weak and *disgust* is too strong. (And it should be disgust *at* something not *of*.) In the second sentence, these words are not well chosen: *tremendous*, *educate*, *activate*.

SELF TEST

Whenever we choose a word, we need to think carefully about the people who are going to read what we have written. For example, suppose you are the captain of a school sports team and you want to say that a team member should be dropped because he or she is not physically strong enough or skilful enough. Which of these words would be suitable for a conversation with **(a)** the headteacher, **(b)** the games teacher, and **(c)** one of your friends? Choose three for each situation.

weak	pansy	feeble	switched off	nerd
dud	drip	ineffectual	laid up	wet
decrepit	wimp	languid	debilitated	pushover
worthless	anorexic	twit	mummy's boy	

Check: *Now check your answers on page 157.*

Writing practice

Now look again at the letter on the previous page. Re-write it using more suitable words. To help you, here are some lists from a thesaurus:

interest

qualms	concern	awareness	anxiety
consciousness	alarm	uneasiness	trouble

disgust

displeasure	anger	revulsion	horror
consternation	offence	contempt	disapproval

tremendous

enormous	ginormous	huge	mega
large-scale	immense	massive	vast

educate

inform	instruct	brief	help to understand
put in the picture	let know	teach	

activate

take action	deal with	move	spare no effort
campaign	go all out	struggle	do one's utmost
do all one can			

Parts of a word

When you are working to improve your vocabulary and spelling, it helps to know how words are made up.

1 **Stem**
  Every word contains a stem. Some words consist of just a stem and nothing else:
  hope

2 **Suffix**
  This is a part that is fixed to the stem and comes **after** it:
  *hope**ful***

3 **Prefix**
  This is a part that is fixed to the stem and comes **before** it:
  ***un**hopeful*

Changing words to fit the sentence

A word stem can also be changed to fit the grammar of the sentence.

1 **Noun plurals**
  Many nouns add ***-s*** to make the plural:
  one book, two books

See pages 100–113 for more on **spelling.**

2 **Verbs – person**
  Verbs change according to the subject:
  I walk, she walks

3 **Verbs – tense**
  Verbs also change to show the difference between tenses:
  I walk, I will walk, I walked

Divide these words into prefix, stem and suffix. Not all the words contain all three.

unhappiness → un+happy+ness

tearful	fortunately	disagreement	enlargement
unexpectedly	hypermarket	overweighty	
regrettable	pro-life	uncleanable	

Check: *Now check your answers on page 157.*

Suffixes

Suffixes are used to make a new word from an existing stem. This often involves changing the class the word belongs to. For example:

beauty (noun) → *beautiful* (adjective)
→ *beautify* (verb)

Commonly used suffixes

1 To make verbs

-ify	beautify
-ise/-ize	advertise

2 To make adjectives

-able/-ible	laughable
-ed	flat-footed
-ful	hateful
-ish	selfish
-less	helpless
-like	child-like

3 To make adverbs

-ly	happily
-wise	clockwise

4 To make nouns

-ant	dependant
-ation/-ion	determination
-ee	employee
-er	employer
-ery/-ry	machinery
-ing	writing
-ment	deferment
-ness	greatness
-ship	leadership

SELF TEST

Use the list of suffixes above to make another word from each of the words in the list:

hood	swift	mine
delight	head	simple
fool	excite	bird
sight	refer	regret

Check: *Now check your answers on page 157.*

Prefixes

Prefixes are used to form new words. They are added to the front of the stem and change its meaning in some way. One of the commonest is *un-*, which gives a word the opposite meaning:

happy → ***un**happy*

These are some of the commonest prefixes, with their meanings:

Prefix	Meaning	Example
ante-	before	antenatal
anti-	against	anti-social
arch-	chief	arch-villain
auto-	self	autobiography
bi-	two	bicycle
circum-	around	circumference
co-	joint, together	co-operate
contra-	opposite	contraflow
counter-	against	counteract
dis-	making the opposite of	disagree
ex-	**1** former **2** out of	ex-teacher extrude
hyper-	very big	hypermarket
im-/in-	**1** opposite of **2** in, into	immature income
inter-	between	international
mega-	very large	megastar
mid-	middle	midfield

Prefix	Meaning	Example
mini-	small	minicomputer
mis-	wrong, false	misplace
mono-	one	monorail
multi-	many	multicoloured
non-	not, opposite of	non-fiction
over-	too much	overtime
post-	after	post-operative
pre-	before	pre-cast
pro-	for	pro-gun
re-	**1** again **2** back	re-write return
self-	self	self-important
semi-	half	semi-circle
sub-	below	submarine
super-	more than, special	superman
tri-	three	tricycle
ultra-	beyond	ultraviolet
un-	not, opposite of	unhelpful
uni-	one	unicycle

1 Try to find an example of your own for each of the following prefixes, then check your answers in a dictionary:

semi-	anti-	ex-
dis-	mini-	auto-
un-	super-	post-

2 Try to work out the meaning of each of these words:

hyperactive	ultrasonic	circumnavigate
megaphone	autosuggestion	contra-indication

Check: *Now check your answers on page 157.*

Word families

As we have seen, the same word can be turned into a number of different words by adding prefixes and suffixes. For example:

*help → help**ful**, **un**help**ful**, help**less***

If you want to improve your vocabulary it is quite a good idea to think of words belonging to families – like this:

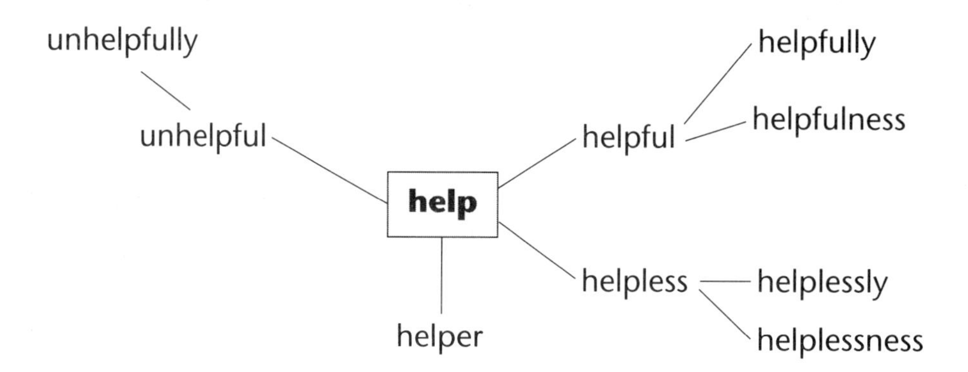

How many words can you think of belonging to the families of each of these word stems:

1 clean
2 large
3 examine?

***Check:** Now check your answers on page 158.*

Writing practice

The writing on the opposite page comes from an examination script. The writer does not show a very wide vocabulary. Re-write and complete the text in a more interesting way. Words and expressions that you might like to change have been circled. Give the description a proper ending, adding new ideas of your own.

When you walk in a supermarket on a busy Saturday morning, you know you won't just be in and out. you will be in there for hours. Your stop by the doors and look around for where to start. All you can see are hundreds of people, families, couples, young students. Most of the children are standing at the music and magazine sections awaiting for their parents to say 'yes' to they can have a new C.D or the latest edition of 'Just Seventeen'.

You can see mothers trying to whizz around the shop picking up anything half price, just so they can get out of the shop.

Young teenagers are pushing the trolleys around for their parents, banging into other trolleys as they try to turn the corner of the aisle.

Rows of trolleys stand in single file along by the checkout counter, all the people looking at their watches wondering how long it will take the

Spelling

English spelling is not easy, but some people find it more difficult than others. Spelling is often something that lets down students who are otherwise very competent writers.

SELF TEST

Look at the extract on the opposite page from a piece of coursework and see how many spelling mistakes you can pick out. For each one, write:

- the line number
- the word as it appears in the answer
- the correct spelling – **without looking it up!**

Check: *Now check your answer on page 158.*

1 *formally known as Mog. When it says, 'The catridge fell invitingly back into the breach,' you knew that the old man wanted it for himself.*

'Educating Rita' is a script with to main characters, both of

5 *these characters have very different backgrounds. Frank is a professor of english litrature who comes from a middle class family and acts accordingly. Rita is a hairdresser who is trying to better herself by taking english litrature. Frank is made her tutor after she enrols in the open university where Frank is working.*

10 *Scene six begins with Rita excitidly running into Frank's office. Frank is obviously worried about why she may wish to burst in to his office, after he is told that nothing's wrong he appears upset, this may be because his life is dull and boring and does not seem to be going any where, but it is more likly that he did not like worring*

15 *without just cause. Rita goes on to tell him that she had gone to see a play and had excitidly enjoyed it. Frank then shows Rita the correct use of the word tragedy, and the diffrence between this and tragic. All the way through the scene you are exposed to the loud pronunciation of Rita, this shows that unlike Frank a distinct lack of 'propper'*

20 *middle class English education was given to her, resulting in slang and abbreviated words not common in the dictionary. The most likely cause of this was spending most of her life in London surrounded by a working class population where crossing your Ts and dotting your Is didn't really matter. Frank also takes the opportunity to invite Rita*

25 *to a dinner party which she reluctantly excepts.*

Why do people make mistakes?

Spelling mistakes aren't just a simple matter of 'getting it wrong'. We make them for several different reasons:

1. **Writing it as you say it**
   With many simple words you can work out how to spell them from the way in which they are spoken: 'c-a-t spells cat'. But if we try this approach with other words, it doesn't work. It isn't *yot*, it's *yacht* and when you do your GCSE it will be an *examination* not an *igzamineyshun*.

2. **Swapping letters round**
   It is very easy, especially when you are in a hurry, to get the order of letters in a word wrong – to write *recieve* instead of *receive*, for example. Often such mistakes are a result of carelessness rather than ignorance.

3. **Missing a letter out**
   Similarly it is easy to miss out a letter, especially when a word contains double letters – to write *adress* instead of *address*, for example.

4. **Putting a letter in**
   If you are not sure about a word that contains single and double letters, you may find that you put in extra letters that should not be there – writing *sherriff* instead of *sheriff*, for example.

5. **Confusing two words**
   There are many pairs of words in English that sound the same or almost the same but are spelled differently. This is a common cause of error. Sometimes these confusing words even come in threes:

   to/two/too and *there/their/they're.*

1. Look through some of your recent pieces of writing in which spelling mistakes have been corrected. Count up how many belong to each of the five groups in the list above. Does this tell you anything about particular problem areas?
2. Go through the same work and list any words that you have written incorrectly more than twice. Which group or groups do these belong to?

Spelling survival programme

The most useful spelling rules and advice on how to tackle the commonest problems come later in this chapter. First you need to work out a personal spelling survival programme:

1 **Get as clear an idea as you can of what your problems are.**
Doing the two activities at the bottom of page 102 will help. Add to those lists any other words or groups of words that you find difficult to spell.

2 **Keep a spelling list in a notebook.**
Allow one or more pages for each letter of the alphabet. Write the correct spellings of difficult words as you come across them, using the correct page of your notebook. Keeping the list in alphabetical order will help you find words easily.

3 **Always use a dictionary.**
Keep it beside you when you write.

4 **Use LOOK – COVER – SPELL – WRITE – CHECK**
If there is a word you are having problems with:
- **look** at the correct spelling carefully
- **cover** it up
- **spell** it out to yourself
- **write** it out
- **check** that you have got it right.

Get into the habit of doing this.

Spelling rules

Rules for changing words

Adding *-s*

We add *-s* to words for two reasons:

- to make nouns plural
- to form the she/he form of the present tense of verbs.

The rules for both are the same, so the plural **-s** rules are given here. Normally you just add **-s**, but there are many exceptions:

1 **Words that end with -ch, -s, -sh, -x, -z**
add ***-es***:
branches, taxes

2 **Words that end in -f or -fe**
change the ending to ***-ves***:
halves, loaves
Exceptions: *beliefs, chiefs, dwarfs, griefs, gulfs, proofs, roofs*

3 **Words that end in vowel + y**
add ***-s***:
ways, buoys

4 **Words that end in consonant + y**
change the ***-y*** to ***-ies***:
poppies

5 **Words that end in -o**
usually just add ***-s***:
radios
Exceptions: *buffaloes, dominoes, echoes, grottoes, haloes, heroes, mangoes, mosquitoes, potatoes, tomatoes, tornadoes, torpedoes, volcanoes*

Cover the rules above and write the plural forms of these words:

piano	half	key	shoe	taxi	cutlass
bush	baby	wrinkle	tax	hero	roof

Check: *Now check your answers on page 159.*

Adding *-ing* and *-ed*

When using verbs, we often need to add the grammatical suffixes ***-ing*** and ***-ed*** to the stem of the verb. Usually you just add ***-ing*** or ***-ed***, but there are a many exceptions:

1. Verbs of one syllable which end with the letter ***e*** and have a long vowel sound (like *rake*), remove the ***-e*** before adding ***-ing*** or ***-ed***:
   raking, raked
   Exceptions are *ageing, queued, queueing*
2. Words of one syllable containing a short vowel sound and ending in a single consonant letter (like *slip*), double the final consonant before adding ***-ing*** or ***-ed***:
   slipping, slipped
3. Words of more than one syllable ending with a single consonant and which you pronounce with the emphasis on the last syllable (like *refer*), double the final consonant and add ***-ing*** or ***-ed***:
   referring, referred
4. Words of more than one syllable ending with a single consonant and which you pronounce with the emphasis on any other syllable (like *benefit*), add ***-ing*** or ***-ed***:
   benefiting, benefited
5. Words ending in a single vowel followed by ***-l*** (like *impel*), double the ***-l*** and add ***-ing*** or ***-ed***:
   impelling, impelled
6. Words ending in two vowels followed by ***-l*** (like *conceal*), add ***-ing*** or ***-ed***:
   concealing, concealed
7. Words ending in a consonant + ***y*** (like *pry*), change the ***-y*** to ***-i*** before ***-ed***:
   pry becomes *prying* and *pried*
8. Words ending in vowel + ***y*** (like *play*), add ***-ing*** or ***-ed***:
   playing, played
   Exceptions: *say/said, pay/paid, lay/laid*

Cover the rules above and write the correct *-ing* and *-ed* forms of each of these verbs:

repel	try	reveal	pay	happen	peel
queue	tape	tip	defer	sharpen	budget

Check: *Now check your answers on page 159.*

Adding *-ly*

Many adjectives can be turned into adverbs by adding ***-ly***. Usually you just add ***-ly*** to the adjective. There are a few exceptions:

1 If the word ends in ***-ll*** (like *full*), just add ***-y***:
fully

2 If the word ends in ***-y*** but has more than one syllable, remove the ***-y*** and add ***-ily***:
happily

3 *Gay* becomes *gaily*.

Adding *-er* and *-est*

Many adjectives can have ***-er*** and ***-est*** added to them:
great, greater, greatest

Usually you just add ***-er*** or ***-est***. There are four groups of exceptions:

1 Words that end in a consonant followed by ***-y*** (like *happy*), change the ***-y*** to an ***-i*** before adding ***-er*** or ***-est***:
happier, happiest

2 Words of one syllable which end with ***-e***, and have a long vowel sound (like *late*), remove the ***-e*** before adding ***-er*** or ***-est***:
later, latest

3 Words of one syllable containing a short vowel sound and ending in a single consonant letter (like *sad*), double the final consonant before adding ***-er*** or ***-est***:
sadder, saddest

4 *Cruel* becomes *crueller* and *cruellest*.

1 Cover the rules above and change each of these adjectives into an adverb by adding *-ly*:

hopeful	recent	fortunate	beautiful
shy	dull	dotty	sure

2 Cover the rules above and write the *-er* and *-est* forms of these words:

quick	dry	sane
small	mad	cruel

Check: *Now check your answers on page 159.*

Other rules

i before *e* except after *c* when the sound is long *ee*

Examples: *thief*, *receive*
Exceptions: *caffeine*, *codeine*, *counterfeit*, *protein*, *seize*, *species*, (plus *either* and *neither*, in some people's pronunciation)

c noun, *s* verb

Which is the noun and which is the verb: *practice* or *practise*?
If it's a noun it's spelled with a ***c***. If it's a verb it's spelled with an ***s***.

Examples:	**verb**	**noun**
	practise	practice
	prophesy	prophecy

-*ise*, -*ize*, -*yse*

Quite a large group of words can be spelled in more than one way.

-ise/-ize
You can spell almost all these words ***-ise***, with the exception of *capsize*.

-yse
This is used for a small group of words which come from Greek. The commonest ones are *analyse* and *paralyse*. You just have to learn these.

-*able*, -*ible*

You will probably just have to learn these, too! Two helpful guidelines are:

1 If it's a new word (like *surfable*) then it will be spelled ***-able***.

2 If you remove ***-able*** from a word, you are usually still left with a complete word. If you do the same with ***-ible***, generally you are not.

-*ar*, -*er*, -*or*

1 We can add ***-er*** to a verb to make a noun, meaning 'the person who does this' (like *designer*)
If the verb already ends in ***-e***, just add ***-r***:
miner
All new nouns made from verbs work in this way.

2 There are a few words that add ***-or*** instead:
actor, *creator*, *inspector*, *sailor*, *visitor*

3 There are also a few that add ***-ar***:
beggar, *burglar*, *liar*

Seeing double

A common problem area is words with one or more pairs of letters the same. The best way to tackle these is to learn them with words that behave in the same way. That is how they are listed here. They are grouped in blocks of five so that you can learn them five at a time.

No double letters

fulfil (*but* fulfilled)	imitate	patrol (*but* patrolled)
marvel (*but* marvelled)	omit (*but* omitted)	pedal (*but* pedalled)
transmit (*but* transmitted)		

One pair of double letters

abbreviate	commit	millionaire	tomorrow
accelerate	corridor	necessary	tranquillity
accident	desiccated	occasion	
accomplish	disappear	occur (but occurred)	
accurate	disappoint	paraffin	
allergy	dissatisfied	parallel	
appropriate	discuss	proceed	
approximate(ly)	exaggerate	procession	
assist	excellent	professional	
beginning	gorilla	questionnaire	
brilliant	happen(ed)	scissors	
caterpillar	harass	sheriff	
collapse	hallelujah	succeed	
collect	illustrate	sufficient	
commemorate	immediate	terrible	

Two pairs of double letters

accommodation	committed	mattress	unnecessary
accidentally	embarrass	millennium	woollen
address	guerrilla	possess	
commission	happiness	successful	

Tricky customers

Then there are those words that just cause problems! This is a list of words that are often spelled incorrectly.

abscess	beautiful	course
absence	because	criticism
achievement	beginning	debt
acknowledgement	behaviour	deceit
acquaintance	believe	deceive
acquiesce	beneficial	definite/definitely
acquire	benefit/benefited	deliberately
across	biscuit	different
adequate	Britain	disagree
advertisement	building	disappear
aeroplane	business	discipline
aisle	canoe/canoeing	enormous
always	catalogue	enthusiasm
amateur	cemetery	especially
amount	chaos	exaggerate
analysis	character	exceptional
anonymous	chief	excitement
anxiety	cigarette	existence
apology	college	expense
arrival	column	extraordinary
ascent	comparatively	extremely
atmosphere	compulsory	favourite
awful/awfully	condemn	February
bargain	conspiracy	ferociously
basically	correspondence	fierce

finally
foreign
forty
friends
further

grammar
guarantee
humorous
hypocrisy
immediately

important
information
interrupt
intrigue
irrelevant

jealousy
jeopardy
knowledge
language
leisure

library
magnificent
maintenance
manoeuvre
marriage

melancholy
naturally
negotiate
neither
ninety

obedient
offered
opinion
opportunity
opposition

ordinary
originally
outrageous
overrule
paid

parliament
particularly
peculiar
perceive
permanent

permission
permitted
persistent
piece
precede

preference
preferred
prejudice
preparation
pretentious

prevalent
privilege
probably
psychiatrist
psychology

pursue
questionnaire
receive
reference
refrigerator

regularly
relieved
religious
remember
reminiscence

responsible
rhythm
ridiculous
schedule
sentence

separate
severely
silhouette
similar
similarly

simultaneous
sincerely
soliloquy
specimen
sponsored

supersede
surprise
sympathy
tragedy
unconscious

undoubtedly
unfortunately
unnecessarily
until
usually

vacuum
vehicle
vicious
view
yesterday

Words commonly confused

Sometimes people don't so much spell words wrongly as use the wrong word. These two lists contain the words most commonly confused. List A contains the more common words. If you don't know the meanings or uses of any of the words, they are all explained in the list of common errors in Chapter 6 starting on page 114.

List A

accept/except
affect/effect
all ready/already
all together/altogether
all ways/always
allowed/aloud
clothes/cloths
fair/fare
have/of
hear/here
knew/new
lay/lie
lead/led
loose/lose
maybe/may be
no/know
passed/past
peace/piece
practice/practise
quiet/quite
read/red
their/there/they're
threw/through
to/too/two
waste/waist
weather/wether/whether
were/we're/where
who's/whose
your/you're

List B

access/excess
advice/advise
allusion/illusion
ascent/assent
board/bored
born/borne
breath/breathe
calendar/colander
canvas/canvass
cereal/serial
check/cheque
choose/chose
cite/sight/site
council/counsel
curb/kerb
currant/current
dependant/dependent
desert/dessert
ensure/insure
gaol/goal
knead/need
licence/license
lightening/lightning
loath/loathe
meter/metre
miner/minor
precede/proceed
principle/principal
stationary/stationery

Single or double?

Without looking back in the book, write out these words correctly. The letters needed to fill the spaces are given, but you have to decide whether one or two of each is needed.

Word	Letters	Word	Letters
a...e...erate	c l	i...itate	m
a...o...odation	c m	ma...ress	t
a...re...	d s	mi...ennium	l
a...i...t	s s	ne...e...ary	c s
be...i...ing	g n	o...asion	c
bri...iant	l	o...it	m
ca...erpi...ar	t l	pa...a...el	r l
co...apse	l	pe...al	d
co...ect	r	po...e...	s s
co...it	m	pro...e...ional	f s
co...idor	r	she...i...	r f
di...a...ear	s p	su...icient	f
emba...a...	r s	te...ible	r
exa...erate	g	u...ece...ary	n s
go...i...a	r l	woo...en	l
ha...a...	r s		

Check: *Now check your answers on page 159.*

SELF TEST

In these sentences there are one or two blanks, followed by two or three words in brackets. Which is the correct word for each blank?

1. I like all my teachers ...... (accept/except) Mrs Brown.
2. ...... (Their/There/They're) are 28 people in our class.
3. I'm not sure ...... (weather/wether/whether) to go for a swim.
4. English elections are organised on a system that is sometimes called 'first ...... (passed/past) the post'.
5. I had flu last month; all I wanted to do was ...... (lay/lie) down.
6. As soon as I got as far as the cinema I ...... (knew/new) I should ...... (have/of) stayed at home.
7. I told her if she didn't hang on to her bag she'd ...... (loose/lose) it.
8. It's good to see the family ...... (all together/altogether) at Christmas.
9. He shouldn't have eaten that second ice cream; I knew it would ...... (affect/effect) him like that.
10. ...... (Who's/Whose) your friend?
11. In the field she found an old ...... (canvas/canvass) bag.
12. That was the year he lost his driving ...... (licence/license).
13. The boat started to leak and they had to ...... (bail/bale) all the time.
14. Their garden looks just like a building ...... (cite/sight/site).
15. Their neighbours have written to the ...... (council/counsel) about it.
16. I must write that date on the ...... (calendar/colander) in the kitchen.
17. She wasn't looking ...... (were/we're/where) she was going and she rode her bike straight into a ...... (stationary/stationery) car.
18. Fortunately she was only 500 ...... (meters/metres) from the accident and emergency department.
19. The birthday cake was as heavy as ...... (lead/led); it ...... (kneaded/needed) some ...... (lightening/lightning).
20. On the way home she tripped over the ...... (curb/kerb).

Check: *Now check your answers on page 160*. All the words in questions 1–10 were from list **A** on page 111. Nearly all those in questions 11–20 were from list **B**.

Common errors

This is a list (in alphabetical order) of the errors examiners and teachers frequently find in students' writing. You will find it useful to read through this list and complete the self-tests to make sure that you have a clear understanding of what each word means.

When your teacher or tutor rings an error in your work, it's worth checking this list to see whether the word is included here. The explanation here should help you to understand how to get it right next time.

accept/except	These are sometimes confused. The meanings of these are shown in this sentence: *I cannot accept that you told everyone except me.*
access/excess	These are sometimes confused. *Access* means the way into somewhere, or the ability to get into somewhere; *excess* means 'too much of something' or 'more than the normal amount'.
advice/advise	These are sometimes confused. *Advice* is a noun; *advise* is a verb.
affect/effect	These are sometimes confused. *Affect* means 'to change something', *effect* means 'the result of a change'. *Effect* also means 'to make something happen'.
all ready/already	These are sometimes confused. *'Are we **all** ready?' asked Mrs Brownlow. 'Yes,' said James, 'and Peter has **already** been sick.'*
all together/altogether	These are sometimes confused. *'Let's go **all together**,' suggested Jason. 'I don't think that's **altogether** a good idea,' replied Miriam.*
all ways/always	These are sometimes confused. *Always* means 'forever'; *all ways* means 'in every way'.
allowed/aloud	These are sometimes confused. *Allowed* means 'permitted'; *aloud* is the opposite of 'silently'.

allusion/illusion

These are sometimes confused. An *allusion* is when you make a mention of something; an *illusion* is when someone has a false or imagined version of the truth.

among/between

These two words are sometimes misused. Normally, we use *between* if there are only two things and *among* if there are more than two:

She divided the sweets ***between*** *the two children.*

She shared the cake ***among*** *all five adults.*

But if you are describing the position of something or exactly how something is arranged, you use *between*:

There is an agreement ***between*** *Mary, Andrew, Ian and me.*

Essex is ***between*** *Suffolk, Hertfordshire, the Thames Estuary and the North Sea.*

and

Some people say that you should not use *and* as the first word in a sentence. Writers have been doing this since Shakespeare's time. The King James Bible uses *and* to start paragraphs. As with many things, used too often, it can become irritating.

One thing you should definitely avoid, is using *and* too often; this is what young children do before they have a full grasp of the language:

We went to see granny ***and*** *she gave us some cakes* ***and*** *we went down to the playing field* ***and*** *we went on the swings ...*

Don't forget that when you make up a compound subject using ***and***, you must make the verb plural:

The new headteacher, Mrs Green, and the long-suffering school secretary, Mrs Bowden, ***is*** *going ...*

Here there are two people, Mrs Green and Mrs Bowden, so the verb should be ***are*** *going*.

are/is	(See **singular** and **plural** on page 125.)
as	This small word can cause problems because it has a number of different meanings, including: 1 while/when 2 because/since The first two can sometimes be confused. For example: ***As*** *I was going to the shops, I decided to buy some onions.* Does the writer mean: 'I made the decision on the way to the shops'? If so, it would be better to write: ***While*** *I was going to the shops, I decided to buy some onions.* If it means that the person decided to buy some onions because they were going to the shops, then it would be better to say so: ***Because*** *I was going to the shops, I decided to buy some onions.* Another problem happens if you use … ***as*** … ***as*** …: *I have visited Peter* ***as*** *often* ***as*** *Mary.* This could mean: *I have visited Peter as often as I have visited Mary.* or *I have visited Peter as often as Mary has.*
ascent/assent	These are sometimes confused. *Ascent* means 'a climb'; *assent* means 'agreement'.

Which of the two words in brackets is correct to fill the spaces in these sentences?

1 She told me that she couldn't (advice/advise) me.
2 I shared the presents (among/between) the thirty children in the class.
3 I just cannot (accept/except) what you are saying.
4 The warning had no (affect/effect) on her.
5 The team thought they were going to win, but it was an (allusion/illusion).

Check: *Now check your answers on page 160.*

between/among	(See **among** on page 115.)
board/bored	These are sometimes confused. A *board* is a piece of wood; *bored* is when you are completely uninterested in something.
born/borne	These are sometimes confused. A baby is *born*; a load is *borne* (or carried).
both/and	*Both* is used to join two things and not more than two. It is wrong, therefore, to write: ***Both** Eleanor **and** the two girls ...* If it has to work with another word, then *both* should work with *and*. So this sentence is wrong: *The team defeated **both** Highbridge **as well as** Wilton.* If you use *both* with figures, it can cause problems, too: ***Both** books cost £20.* Did each book cost £10 or £20? Better to write either: *Each book cost £10.* or *The two books together cost £40.*

breath/breathe	These are sometimes confused. *Breath* is a noun; *breathe* is a verb.
calendar/colander	These are sometimes confused. A *calendar* is for dates; a *colander* is for vegetables.
canvas/canvass	These are sometimes confused. *Canvas* is a material; during an election, political parties *canvass* - they ask people if they will vote for them.
cereal/serial	These are sometimes confused. A *cereal* is a type of grain like wheat - and what many people eat for breakfast; a *serial* is a group of things that happen in order (series), like the episodes of a soap.
check/cheque	These are sometimes confused. To *check* is to make sure about something; a *cheque* is a piece of paper with which you pay money from your bank account.
choose/chose	These are sometimes confused. *Chose* is the past tense of *choose*: *They said I would have to* ***choose****, so I* ***chose*** *the smallest one I could see.*
cite/site/sight	These are sometimes confused. *Cite* means 'quote'; a *site* is a place; a *sight* is something you see.
clothes/cloths	These are sometimes confused. *Clothes* are what you wear; *cloths* are pieces of material: *clothes* are usually made of *cloth*.
collective nouns	Collective nouns are singular nouns that describe groups of people: the police, the government, the public, and so on. The problem is, do you use a singular or a plural verb with them? Which is correct? *The government is to blame*, or *The government are to blame*? The answer is that often both are possible. If you are thinking of the subject as a single thing, then use a singular verb. (Most of the time we think of the government as a single thing, so we use a singular verb.) If you think of the subject as a number of individuals, then use a plural verb: *The police have made a number of arrests.*

Sometimes either can be used without much difference in meaning:

The public is requested to keep off the grass
The public are requested to keep off the grass.

council/counsel

These are sometimes confused. A *council* is a group of people, often elected, who meet to make decisions about things; *counsel* means 'advice' and a counsel is a lawyer (who advises and speaks for a client).

curb/kerb

These are sometimes confused. A *curb* is something that holds someone or something back; a *kerb* runs along the edge of a pavement.

currant/current

These are sometimes confused. A *currant* is a dried fruit; you find *currents* in the sea or in large lakes. *Current* also means 'happening at this moment, up-to-date'.

There are many strong currants in this part of the ocean.

dependant/dependent

These are sometimes confused. *Dependant* is a noun; *dependent* is an adjective.

desert/dessert

These are sometimes confused. *Dessert* means 'pudding'; *desert(s)* means what a person deserves – *their just deserts*. *Desert* also means an arid place, or 'to abandon'.

disinterested/ uninterested

These are sometimes confused. *Disinterested* means 'not taking sides'; *uninterested* means 'bored'.

each	When you use each on its own, remember that it is singular and requires a singular verb: *Each of the players* ***has*** *one shot at goal.* (not *Each* … ***have*** …)
e.g./i.e.	These have different meanings and should not be confused. *e.g.* means 'for example'; *i.e.* means 'that is' or 'in other words'. Note the punctuation of each.
ensure/insure	These are sometimes confused. *Ensure* means to 'make sure that something happens'; if you *insure* against something happening, you make preparations against it. So, for example you *insure* your car by paying for an insurance policy, so that if you have a crash, you won't have to pay the costs.
even	This common adverb can cause confusion if you put it in the wrong place in a sentence. All these sentences have different meanings: 1 ***Even*** *the scientists are concerned about traffic fumes.* 2 *The scientists are* ***even*** *concerned about traffic fumes.* 3 *The scientists are concerned about* ***even*** *traffic fumes.* 1 means that everyone, including scientists, is concerned 2 means that scientists are concerned about lots of things, including traffic fumes 3 means that scientists are concerned about all fumes, including traffic fumes. To avoid confusion, *even* should be placed next to the word it refers to.

Some of these sentences have mistakes in them. Which sentences, and what is the mistake?

1 The father did not hear the news until several hours after his daughter was born.
2 She told me she'd left the carrots in the calendar to drain.
3 The teacher blamed both me and my two friends Dean and Wayne.
4 The public is not allowed beyond this point.
5 She has just been elected to the local counsel.

Check: *Now check your answers on page 160.*

fair/fare

These are sometimes confused.

*It's not **fair** that students who forget their bus passes have to pay the full **fare**.*

fewer/less

If the thing you are talking about is something you can count - like matches or people - then you should use 'fewer':

*There were **fewer** people on the picket line than yesterday.*
(not ... ***less*** *people* ...)

If the thing cannot be counted - like butter, or success - then you use *less*:

*The strikers had **less** success today than they did yesterday.*

gaol/goal

These are sometimes confused. *Gaol* is a 'prison' (pronounced the same as *jail*); a *goal* is a 'target'.

have/of

These are sometimes confused. People say and write *I could/should/might **of*** ... when they mean *I could/should/might **have*** ...

hear/here

These are sometimes confused. If you listen, you *hear*; *here* means 'in this place'.

I/me

It is a common mistake to use *I* instead of *me* in sentences like this:

*That CD was given to my sister and **I** at Christmas.*

This should be:

*... to my sister and **me** ....*

(Think about it this way: you wouldn't say, ... *was given to I* ..., would you?)

The rule is that you use *I* as the subject of a verb: ***I*** *like curry.*

If it is the object of the verb, it is ***me***:

*Unfortunately, curry doesn't like **me**.*

If it comes after a preposition, it is *me*:

*She gave it to **me** as a present.*

i.e.	(See ***e.g.*** on page 120.)
is/are	(See **singular and plural** on page 125.)
its/it's	These sometimes cause difficulty. Remember: *its* means of it *it's* is the short form of it is, it has
knead/need	These are sometimes confused. *If you are making bread, you **need** to **knead** the dough.*
knew/new	These are sometimes confused. *I **knew** I would lose my **new** coat if I took it to school.*
lay/lie	These are sometimes confused. The present tense is: *When you go to bed, you **lie** down.* The past tense of this is: *When you went to bed you **lay** down.* The problem is that *lay* is also a verb in its own right: chickens *lay* eggs. The past tense of *lay* is *laid*.
lead/led	These are sometimes confused. *Lead* has two meanings and two pronunciations. It can be pronounced to rhyme with 'heed', when it means 'to be in front'. If it is pronounced to rhyme with 'bed', it means a heavy (and poisonous) metal. *Led* is the past tense of *lead* when it rhymes with 'heed'.
licence/license	These are sometimes confused. *Licence* is a noun; *license* is a verb.
lightening/lightning	These are sometimes confused. We say ***lightning*** *never strikes twice in the same place* (not, in fact, true). If a cake mixture is heavy, it needs to be made lighter - it needs ***lightening***.
loath/loathe	These are sometimes confused. *Loath* is an adjective; *loathe* is a verb.

loose/lose

These are sometimes confused. *If you let your pet dog run **loose**, you may **lose** it.*

may/might

People often use *may*, when they should use *might*. We use *may* for things that are still possible and *might* for things that are very unlikely. Compare these two sentences:

1 *By losing last night, the team **may** have ruined their chances of becoming champions.*

2 *If they had not kept their nerve, the team **might** have ruined their chances of becoming champions.*

1 means that they may or may not still become champions - we don't know

2 means that the speaker thinks they will probably still become champions and that they have not ruined their chances.

maybe/may be

These are sometimes confused. *Maybe* means 'perhaps'; *may be* is part of a verb phrase. *What you have said **may be** true. **Maybe** we should do something about it.*

meter/metre

These are sometimes confused. A *meter* is used for measuring (e.g. an electricity meter); a *metre* is a distance made up of 100 centimetres. It is also the word used to describe the regular rhythm of some poetry.

miner/minor

These are sometimes confused. A *miner* digs underground; a *minor* is a person under the age of maturity (usually 18 years).

no/know	These are sometimes confused. *You should **know** that when I say '**no**', I mean '**no**'!*
only	This common adverb can cause confusion if you put it in the wrong place in a sentence. Compare these four sentences: 1 ***Only the librarian** should remove books from shelves* (i.e. no one else should remove books). 2 *The librarian should **only remove** books from shelves* (i.e. the librarian should not put them back on the shelves; someone else should). 3 *The librarian should remove **only books** from shelves* (i.e. the librarian should not remove records or magazines from the shelves). 4 *The librarian should remove books **only from shelves*** (i.e. the librarian should not remove books from places other than shelves, such as tables or windowsills).
passed/past	These are sometimes confused. *Passed* is part of the verb 'pass'. *If you pass by someone, you have just gone **past** them.* *Julie has **passed** her exam.*
peace/piece	These are sometimes confused. *Peace* is the opposite of war; a *piece* is a part of something.

Some of these sentences have mistakes in them. Which sentences, and what is the mistake?

1 This strange man came up to my mother and I as we were going to the supermarket.
2 The flu is spreading; there were less people in school today.
3 It's a shame that the team has lost its place in the league.
4 The two posts were about fifty meters apart.
5 She was so tired she just lay down fully dressed and fell asleep … .

***Check:** Now check your answers on page 160.*

practice/practise	These are sometimes confused. *Practice* is a noun; *practise* is a verb.
precede/proceed	These are sometimes confused. *Precede* means 'go before, or in front of'; *proceed* means 'go along'.
principle/principal	These are sometimes confused. *Principle* means the idea or truth that underlies something, for example *The Guiding Principle of a person's life*. The *Principal* of a college is its head, and as an adjective *principal* means 'chief' or 'main'.
quiet/quite	These are sometimes confused. *Quiet* is the opposite of 'noisy'; *quite* means 'rather'.
read/red	Sometimes people confuse these two in sentences like this: *Have you (read/red) 'The Maltese Falcon?'* This is because the correct word read is pronounced in the same way as 'red'. Remember that the verb *to read* is an irregular verb and doesn't change when you move from the present to the past: ***present:*** *I read (now)* ***past:*** *I read (then)* ***perfect:*** *I have read.*
singular and plural	*Singular* means one of something; *plural* means more than one. If the subject of a sentence is singular, then you have a singular verb: *Jane **was** at the cinema last night with Dave.* If the subject is plural, then the verb must be plural: *Jane and Dave **were** at the cinema last night.* Problems arise when the subject is long and complicated: *Several of my old school friends, including Jane, was/were at the cinema last night.* Ask yourself, *How many people: one or more than one?* Here the answer is 'more than one' so the verb should be 'were'. (See also **Checking agreement** on page 40.)

so	*so* can produce confusions similar to those of *as*, because it can mean: • 'as a result' • 'in order that'. This sentence, for example, is ambiguous: *He left home so his parents could get some peace.* To make the meaning clear it should be rephrased; in one of two ways: • *He left home **in order that** his parents could get some peace.* • *He left home and **as a result** his parents could get some peace.*

stationary/stationery	These are sometimes confused. *Stationary* is an adjective and means 'standing still'; *stationery* is paper, envelopes, and other things that can be bought at a stationer's.
taught/taut	These are sometimes confused. Subjects are *taught* in schools; *taut* means 'tight, not loose'.
their/there/they're	These are sometimes confused. *Their* means 'belonging to them'; *there* is often contrasted with 'here'; *they're* is a short form of 'they are'.

threw/through	These are sometimes confused. *Threw* is the past tense of 'throw'; *through* is a preposition: *She fell* ***through*** *a hole in the ice.*
to/too/two	These are sometimes confused. *To* is often contrasted with 'from' (***to*** *and from school*); *too* means *also*; one and one make *two*.
was/were	(See **singular and plural** on page 125.)
waste/waist	These are sometimes confused. *Waste* is 'rubbish'; people's *waists* come about half way down their bodies.
weather/whether/ wether	These are sometimes confused. The *weather* forecast tells us *whether* it is going to rain or not; a *wether* is a sheep.
were/was	(See **singular and plural** on page 125.)
were/we're/where	These are sometimes confused. *Were* is the past tense of 'are'; *we're* is a short form of 'we are'; *where* is, among other things, a question word meaning 'in what place?'
who's/whose	These are sometimes confused. *Who's* is short for 'who is'; *whose* means 'belonging to whom'.
your/you're	These are sometimes confused. *Your* means 'belonging to you'; *you're* is a short form of 'you are'.

The writer of these sentences has chosen a number of wrong words. What are they and what should they be?

1 I was delighted when I red that you have finally past your exam.
2 Popular sayings include: 'Practise makes perfect' and 'To heads are better than one'.
3 In bad wether it's difficult to know wether to take an umbrella or a raincoat.
4 Outside the stationery shop there was a waste removal vehicle, which was stationary, but as I arrived it drove off.
5 Dave through me a book, but I don't know who's it was.

Check: *Now check your answers on page 160.*

7 Reference

This chapter gives you a brief explanation of terms you may come across in your English lessons. If the term is explained at length in earlier chapters of this book, you will find a short explanation here and/or a page reference for its earlier explanation. If the term does not appear elsewhere in the book, you will find a full explanation here.

If you find a word that is underlined, this means that the word has its own entry in this section, where you will find a fuller explanation.

abbreviation	An abbreviation is any short form of a word or group of words, like a name or title. Abbreviations sometimes turn into words in their own right and then they are called acronyms. (There is more about ABBREVIATIONS on page 76.)
abstract noun	A noun which refers to an idea, thought, emotion or something else that cannot be touched, tasted, seen, heard, or smelled.
acronym	An abbreviation that is used as if it were a normal word, such as NATO. The letters of such abbreviations do not need to be followed by full stops. (There is more about ACRONYMS on pages 64 and 76.)
adjective	Adjectives are words that: • work with nouns to change, or add to their meaning: *She saw a **tall, slender, unhappy** woman standing at the door.* • can be used with linking verbs to complete a sentence: *Damon is **happy.*** • can often have a comparative form (*happier*) and a superlative form (*happiest*).
adverb	Adverbs change or add to the meaning of verbs: *She was walking **slowly** down the path.* When they are used with verbs, adverbs answer questions such as: **how?** *She was walking **slowly**.* **how much?** *I love ice cream **enormously**.* **when?** *I'll see you **tomorrow**.* **where?** *There was mud **everywhere.*** **in what direction?** *They were crawling **forwards**.*

	Adverbs also change the meaning of adjectives and adverbs – by answering the question **how much?** • *Gail was* ***very*** *unhappy.* • *She walked back* ***extremely*** *slowly.*
agreement	The subject and the verb of a sentence must agree. If the subject is plural, then the verb, too, must be plural: *Many of my friends, including Brett, like water-skiing.* It would be a mistake to write *likes* here, because the subject is *friends*, not *Brett*. (There is more about AGREEMENT on page 40.)
apostrophe	(There is information about APOSTROPHES on page 66.)
article	A small group of words that work with nouns or noun phrases: *a*, *an*, *the*.
audience	Good writers are aware of the audience they are writing for. Whatever audience you are writing for, there are three main things you need to remember: **1** how well you know them **2** what they know about the subject **3** their age and experience. (There is more about AUDIENCE starting on page 17.)
auxiliary verb	A verb that works with the full verb in a sentence to make a complete verb phrase. Examples are: *be, is, am, are, was, were, have, do, shall, should, will, would, may, might, can, could*. Examples of auxiliary verbs in a verb phrase are: ***was*** *walking*; ***might*** *arrive*; ***would have been*** *sending*. (There is more about AUXULIARY VERBS on page 38.)
brackets	(There is information about BRACKETS on page 72.)
capital letters	(There is information about CAPITAL LETTERS on page 64.)
clause	A group of words that forms a whole simple sentence, or part of a multiple sentence. A clause normally contains a subject and a finite verb. It often also contains other things (for example an object). (There is more about CLAUSES on page 47.)

collective noun	Nouns which refer to groups of people or things are called collective nouns. Common examples are: *community, group, audience, committee, government, team* Although they refer to more than one person or thing, collective nouns can behave as if they were singular: *The army was moving forward at great speed.* The problem is that many of them can be followed by plural verbs as well as singular ones: *The public is requested to respect the Lord's House.* *The public are not allowed beyond this point.* The first sentence sees the public primarily as a single group, but the second sees them as a number of individual people.
colon	(There is information about the COLON on page 70.)
common noun	Nouns are divided into common nouns and proper nouns. The great majority of nouns are common nouns.
comma	(There is information about COMMAS on page 68.)
complex sentence	(See sentence)
compound sentence	(See sentence)
concrete noun	A noun that refers to something we can see, hear, smell, taste, or touch.
conjunction	A word that is used to join **a**) two words, (**b**) two phrases, or **c**) two clauses: (**a**) *bread **and** butter* (**b**) *individual students **or** small groups* (**c**) *Gina is happy **but** Mark is definitely not.*
dash	(There is information about DASHES on page 72.)
direct speech	When we write an account of a conversation quoting the exact words used and enclose them in inverted commas, it is referred to as direct speech. (The rules for punctuating direct speech are given on page 77.)
directive	(There is information about DIRECTIVES on page 33.)

exclamation	(There is information about EXCLAMATIONS on page 33.)
exclamation mark	(There is information about EXCLAMATION MARKS on pages 33 and 63.)
finite verb	Every simple sentence must contain a finite verb, and in a multiple sentence so must every clause. A finite verb: • shows **tense**. *They **walked** home after the disco had ended.* • shows **agreement** between the subject and the verb. *I walk/he walks/they walk.* (There is more about FINITE VERBS on page 36.)
first person	(See person)
formal	(See tone)
full stop	(There is information about FULL STOPS on page 62.)
full verb	A verb that has a dictionary meaning. It can be used on its own: *Pete just **gulped** down his food.* Or it can be used with one or more auxiliary verbs: *He* **has been** ***gulping*** *his food down like that for years.* (There is more about VERBS starting on page 36.)
informal	(See tone)
inverted commas	These can be single ('...') or double ("..."), and are used: • always in pairs • to open and close direct speech. They are placed round the words actually spoken by a character • to begin and end a quotation • to enclose the titles of works in articles, magazines, newspapers, songs, programmes. (There is more about INVERTED COMMAS – QUOTATION MARKS – on page 66.)
linking verb	In some sentences and clauses, the subject and what follows the verb refer to the same person or thing: *Jane is a medical student.* Here the words *Jane* and *medical student* refer to the same person. Verbs used in this kind of sentence are called **linking verbs**. Examples are: *be, seem, appear, become.*
multiple sentence	(See sentence)

narrative	Another word for story. When you write narrative it is important to consider the viewpoint from which the story is told. This is sometimes called **narrative viewpoint**.
noun	It is sometimes said that nouns are the names of persons, places, and things. It is true that the names of persons, places, and things are nouns, but so are a lot of other words, like *happiness* and *conviction*, neither of which is a person, a place, or a thing. Most of the time you will have little difficulty spotting nouns, but if you do, here are some tests you can use. Most nouns (but not all!): • can make a plural by adding ***-s*** • can show possession by adding ***-'s*** to the singular • can have an article (*a*, *an*, *the*) or a similar word in front of them (*the book*, *some happiness*) • can have an adjective before them (***great*** *happiness*) • can be the subject of a sentence (***Happiness*** *is the most important thing in life*). (See also: abstract noun, collective noun, common noun, concrete noun, proper noun)
object	In a statement sentence, the object usually comes after the verb and refers to someone or something that is affected by the verb. *The train struck* ***the buffers***. *Katie licked* ***her ice cream***. The object always refers to a different person or thing from the subject unless it is one of these words: *myself*, *himself*, *herself*, *yourself*, *yourselves*, *ourselves*, *themselves*. *She cut* ***herself*** *while trying to mend her bike.*
paragraph	A piece of writing of any length is usually divided into paragraphs. This makes it easier for readers to find their way through the writing and to understand the main points the writer is making. (There is more about PARAGRAPHS on pages 53 and 74.)
person	Personal pronouns can be: first person: *I*, *we* (and *me* etc.) second person: *you* (and *your* etc.) third person: *she*, *he*, *it*, *they* (and *her* etc.) A 'first person narrative' is an 'I story' - one told as if the storyteller is taking part in the story.

prefix

Part of a word which comes before the stem: ***un****expected*, ***super****market*.
(There is more about PREFIXES on page 96.)

preposition

A group of words that come before a noun (***up*** *country*, ***down*** *town*) or a phrase based on a noun (***up*** *the steep flight of stairs*, ***down*** *a narrow street*).
Common prepositions include:
above, across, at, behind, beside, by, down, from, in, off, on, over, to, under, up

pronoun

A group of words that stand in for other words in a sentence to save too much repetition. As their name suggests, pronouns often stand in for nouns:
I saw Mrs Graham yesterday. ***She*** *was going to the doctor's.*
Sometimes they stand for whole groups of words or ideas that the writer has already mentioned:
The headteacher wants to change the school uniform. ***This*** *is very popular with senior pupils.*
Personal pronouns include:
I, she, we etc.
my, your, their etc.
mine, yours etc.
Other common pronouns include:
this, that etc.
Many pronouns refer back to nouns or noun phrases and this can cause confusion. There are two common causes for this.

- Sometimes it is not clear what earlier part of a text a pronoun refers to, for example if there is more than one thing it could refer to:
  Parents of children who fail to put their names on their possessions should not complain if they lose them.
  Whose names go on the possessions and who loses what? It would be much clearer to write:
  If parents don't put names on their children's possessions, they should not complain if their children lose them.
- Sometimes the writer fails to provide anything for the pronoun to refer to, so that it is left hanging in mid air:
  The company has tried to reduce petty theft in the spares department, but they are still very high.
  Here *they* doesn't refer to anything that has gone before and should be replaced by a suitable noun, *losses*, for example.

proper noun	Proper nouns are the names, of people, places, months, days: words like *John*, *New Zealand*, *January*, *Tuesday*. They are different from other nouns (called common nouns). In particular they don't usually have an article (unless there is one 'built in' - as in *The Hague*) and don't have a plural (unless they are always plural) - you can't talk about 'many New Zealands'.
purpose	When we speak or write we do so for a purpose. For example: • **to interact** (meeting and greeting friends, talking at parties) • **to inform** (textbooks, instruction manuals, some magazines) • **to find out** (asking questions) • **to entertain** (stories, songs) • **to persuade** (advertisements, arguments) • **to control** (laws, notices, school rules) • **to record** (diaries). (There is more about PURPOSE on page 17.)
question	(There is information about QUESTIONS on page 33.)
question mark	(There is information about QUESTION MARKS on page 62.)
quotation marks	(See inverted commas)
relative clause	A clause in a complex sentence which does the job of an adjective. *Those people* ***who are sitting in the corner*** *keep on staring at me.* A relative clause is often introduced by a relative pronoun such as *who*, *whom*, *which*, *that*, *where*, *when*.
script	(There is information about DRAMA SCRIPTS on page 79.)
second person	(See person)
semicolon	This punctuation mark is used: • to join two or more sentences which are linked in subject matter: *All births in Loune have been registered since 1905; the birth of the oldest living inhabitant was registered in 1906.* • to separate items in a list when commas are needed to punctuate phrases describing each item: *The bag contained: a greying battered pair of trainers; one yellow sock and, as its mate could no longer be called yellow, a brown sock.* (There is more about SEMICOLONS on page 70.)

sentence

Sentences can be:

- **simple**
  a simple sentence contains only one finite verb (another way of describing it is to say that it has only one clause): *The cat* ***sat*** *on the mat.*
- **multiple**
  a multiple sentence contains more than one finite verb (it has more than one clause): *The cat* ***sat*** *on the mat and the dog* ***bit*** *it.*
  Multiple sentences can be:
  - **compound**
    a compound sentence is made up of clauses joined together by conjunctions like *and*, *or*, *but*. Each of the clauses is of equal importance: *The cat sat on the mat and the dog bit it.*
    a compound sentence can be split into a series of simple sentences: *The cat sat on the mat. The dog bit it.*
  - **complex**
    In a complex sentence there is one **main** clause and one or more others that are less important. In this example the main clause is in bold type.
    The dog bit the cat *that sat on the mat.*
    The main clause usually works as a sentence on its own: *The dog bit the cat.*
    Subordinate clauses do not usually work on their own: *that sat on the mat.*

(There is more about SENTENCES starting on page 33.)

---

simple sentence

(See sentence)

---

statement

(There is information about STATEMENTS starting on page 33.)

---

stem

If a word has a prefix or a suffix, the stem is the part they are attached to:

PREFIX	STEM	SUFFIX
un	*happi*	*ness*

Here the stem is *happy* (with a spelling change because of the addition of the suffix).

(There is more about SUFFIXES and PREFIXES starting on page 94.)

style

The style of a piece of writing is 'how it reads'. We talk about a text having 'an easy, readable style', or 'a rather formal style'. We also talk about an individual person's style: *That's Kate's* ***style****; I'd recognise it anywhere.*

A writer's style is made up of their choice of vocabulary, how they construct their sentences, how they combine sentences into paragraphs – the total impact of their writing. There isn't much you can do about your style consciously and deliberately, but if you focus on these things you will always write better:

- **subject matter**
  Make sure that you know everything you need to know about the subject and are confident to write about it.
- **audience**
  Think carefully about the audience you are writing for and their particular needs.
- **purpose**
  Be clear in your mind of the purpose for your writing.

---

subject

In a statement sentence, the subject comes at or near the beginning of the sentence, before the verb. It can be one word or a group of words (a phrase). It often tells us what the sentence is going to be about:

Our summer holiday last year *was a disaster.*

but not always:

There is a lot of flu about this winter.

(There is more about SUBJECT on page 34.)

---

suffix

A group of letters coming after the stem of a word. Suffixes are used to form new words:

beauty → beautify

happy → happiness

(There is more about SUFFIXES on page 95.)

---

tense

The form of a verb can give information about *when* and *how* an action takes place:

I walk

I am walking

I walked

I was walking

I shall walk

and so on.

These different forms of the verb are called tenses.

third person — (See person)

tone — We use the word 'tone' to describe the way in which writers address their audience. If you know your audience well, you can use a relaxed informal tone, but if you are writing for people you have never met then you probably need to be more formal. These are some of the things that decide the tone of a piece of writing:

- **vocabulary**
  Words such as *leader*, *senior officer*, *chief*, *principal*, *head* are formal, but *big cheese*, *boss*, *guvnor*, and *big shot* are informal.
- **sentence construction**
  If you are writing a formal letter, you might end by saying *I look forward to hearing from you*. Informally this might become *Give me a bell when you're free*.
- **short forms**
  In informal writing, it is all right to use short forms such as *isn't* and *won't*. In formal writing these should be written out in full: *is not* and *will not*.

verb — We use the word 'verb' in two slightly different ways:

- to describe a class of single words:
  'Green' is an adjective and 'happen' is a verb. In this case a verb is always only one word.
- to describe an essential part of a sentence. For example, the verb in the following sentence is printed in **bold**.
  That poor old woman ***has been waiting*** *at the bus stop for three quarters of an hour.*
  In this case a verb can be one word, or a group of words, a phrase, made up of a full verb and one or more auxiliary verbs.

(There is more about VERBS on page 36.)

viewpoint — A story can be told from a number of different viewpoints. It may be a 'first person' story in which events are described by one of the characters in the story (as 'I'). It may, on the other hand, be a 'third person' story in which all events are described by a storyteller who stands outside the story. A third person story can do one of these three things:

- follow one of the characters all the time, telling the reader all about that character's thoughts and feelings, but only describing

other people as they are seen by that character
- follow one part of the story from one character's viewpoint and then move to another character for the next part
- look down on all the characters 'from a height' and not look into the thoughts and feelings of any of them.

vocabulary	The words used by a writer. We all have two sections to our vocabulary: • **active** vocabulary: the words we are confident about using in our own speech and writing • **passive** vocabulary: the words that we recognise and think we understand, but do not use regularly in our own speech and writing. (There is more about VOCABULARY on page 89.)

8 Answers to self-tests

1 Meet the examiner

page 11: Check with the examiner

Answer A

Does it describe the place well?
This writer isn't sure how to tackle the question and decides to write a letter to the local newspaper explaining why she is writing and asking if her article could be published.

She does not get down to the task itself until the second paragraph and even then she doesn't really know how to go about it. She is very ambitious because she tries to describe the whole village, but only gives a very simple description. There is no real detail and she does not seem to know how to catch the reader's interest. We can see that this writer is struggling to think of something to write about, because the village does not suggest any obvious subject matter to her. On the other hand she mentions a park, some shops, and a street view. Any of these could be a good topic for description.

Is it well organised?
The writer has no real sense of purpose or organisation. The writing is shapeless and thin and, although it is reasonably clear, it is very simple.

Are the sentences clear and is the grammar correct?
The control of sentence construction is very poor. In line 13, for example, there should either be a full stop after 'church' or a conjunction, such as 'and', to link the two parts of the sentence. In line 16 there should be a conjunction between 'village' and 'all'.

Are the sentences properly punctuated?
The punctuation is rather thin and the mistakes are usually linked to mistakes in sentence construction. There are other punctuation mistakes, too. For example, the list in line 9 should have a comma separating the items.

Does the writer use words well and spell them correctly?
The writer misuses or mis-spells words:

Line 2	*serious*	should be	*series*
Line 3	*wouldring*	should be	*wondering*
Line 9	*tress*	should be	*trees*
Line 11	*offers*	should be	*office*

Sometimes it is difficult to tell if these mistakes are mistakes of vocabulary or spelling. For example:

Line 5 *compertensine* should be *competition*

Other mistakes are obviously spelling mistakes:

Line 1	*writting*	should be	*writing*
Line 22	*liveing*	should be	*living*

What grade would you give this piece of writing?
This answer does communicate its meaning in a simple way, but sometimes the reader has to work quite hard to understand it. Even if all the mistakes of grammar, punctuation and spelling were corrected, it would still be rather simple and dull. So the writer needs to give a lot more thought to planning and organising her writing. The writer is struggling to cope with the demands of the task and, although the writing does communicate, it does so at a very basic level. There are many errors.

It is probably at grade F.

Answer B

Does it describe the place well?
The writer shows an immediate sense of purpose and she clearly understands what is required and how to set about the task. She has the idea of exploring what the park means to various people and this gives her writing a focus.

The beginning is rather clever in showing how the park is central to the lives of people in the town. There is neat observation in the details, and the sequence from babies to the elderly shows the significance of this park to the whole community. The various activities which take place in any park are mentioned in relation to specific groups of people. For example, babies being taken for a ride in a pushchair, children playing on the swings or young couples walking together, are all familiar sights and this writer has some powers of observation. It is those touches of convincing detail which make a good piece of description.

Is it well organised?
This piece of writing may not be perfect, but it is very good and part of its quality lies in the observation of the precise details. Some of the details may seem rather obvious or predictable to you but they give the writing some substance and give us a visual sense of the place and the activities which you would find there.

Are the sentences clear and is the grammar correct?
The sentences are absolutely in control. She has no hesitation about using simple sentences and the opening of the piece is a single statement with no elaboration. However, other sentences are longer and more complex. Her writing shows variety and control.

Are the sentences properly punctuated?
The punctuation is accurate and it is used for a purpose. She does not scatter commas around at random and she knows when to use a full stop. She uses the apostrophe when it is necessary, but only when it is necessary.

Does the writer use words well and spell them correctly?
There are some impressive touches in the vocabulary. For example:

haven (line 8), *lush* (line 9), *vibrant* (line 10), *avid* (line 13), *forbidding* (line 15), *myriad* (line 21).

However the writing is not littered with 'big' or 'unfamiliar' words. Much of the vocabulary is common but clearly moving beyond basic or simple words.

The most impressive feature is the fact that words are being used in the right place. The spelling is accurate and there are some words used here which might cause trouble. For example: *families* (line 6), *centre* (line 10), *techniques* (line 14), *happiness* (line 17), *innocent* (line 17), *beautiful* (line 19), *description* (line 20) *surrounding* (line 23).

What grade would you give this piece of writing?
The writer has a clear awareness of what is required and the writing is organised and accurate. There is some ambition in what is attempted and any examiner would reward mechanical skill and the precise observation of details. This writer has something to say and she knows how to say it. The expression is sophisticated and elegant and there is real control and organisation.

This is certainly at the top of the range. It is A/A* quality.

page 14

Answer C

Does it describe the place well?
The writer has a good eye for detail and includes good observations of features in a supermarket. She catches the atmosphere of noise and bustle very effectively and most of us will be familiar with the experiences she is describing. She observes the range of people in the supermarket from shoppers and children to checkout assistants and shelf-fillers, exploring their attitudes and feelings as well as their behaviour.

The final paragraph comments on how commercial society is, and how this is reflected in the shopping patterns of a supermarket. This is ambitious and thoughtful and brings the piece to a neat conclusion.

Is it well organised?
The writing is organised into paragraphs and, overall, it reads well. If it has a weakness it is the impression that she is writing her ideas as they come into her mind, and not working to a clear plan. She is bright enough to get away with it but it is a risk and most writing needs at least some planning to give it shape.

Are the sentences clear and is the grammar correct?
There is complete control here. The writer is confident in using complex sentences such as: *The tasteful relaxing music in the background which flowed out from speakers around the store, was drowned by a wave of young children screaming, the sound of metal attacking metal, the monotonous beeps of the tills and the groaning shoppers* (lines 14–18). Yet she also knows how to use a simple sentence to good effect, such as her final line: *Every Saturday was the same* (line 29).

Are the sentences properly punctuated?
Indeed they are. There is accuracy, confidence, and apparently effortless ease here.

Does the writer use words well and spell them correctly?
The vocabulary is wide and is used correctly. She is particularly careful in her choice of adverbs and adjectives such as *shoppers eagerly tried to push themselves* (line 1) and *tasteful relaxing music* (line 14). There are also some

very neat turns of phrase such as *the colourful temptation of the sweet counter* (line 5).

She spells some words correctly which are notoriously difficult. For example: *ageing* (line 2), *trolleys* (line 3), *favourite* (line 7), *queues* (line 13), *groceries* (line 19), *necessity* (line 23), *exhaustion* (line 24), *commercialism* (line 25).

What grade would you give this piece of writing?

Although the organisation is perhaps not perfect, there are many qualities in this piece of writing. It is accurate and ambitious and any examiner would reward the control of language. The content is interesting, even if it does seem a little shapeless.

This is close to the top of the range. It is A/A* quality.

Answer D

Does it describe the place well?

The writer is obviously writing from personal experience of shopping in supermarkets so the basic ideas are there. However, nothing is developed in any real detail and the final effect is thin. There are a lot of missed opportunities here, where the writer could have used description of the supermarket and observation of how people behave.

Is it well organised?

There is a simple structure in the writing and, although the piece is very undeveloped, there is a sense of shape and basic organisation. It is possible to follow the writing quite easily.

Are the sentences clear and is the grammar correct?

This is where the writer is in serious difficulty. There is no control over sentence construction and the tenses are constantly changing. Many of the errors are very basic. For example, 'their' is misused in lines 2 and 12 and 'your' is wrong in lines 6 and 8. The writing is clumsy in expression and occasionally it makes communication difficult. In line 2 the use of 'shopper' instead of 'shopping' forces the reader to read the sentence again and do some of the writer's work.

Are the sentences properly punctuated?

The punctuation is rather thin and the mistakes are usually linked to mistakes in sentence construction. For example, there should be a full stop after 'shop' in line 5, instead of a comma. The full stop at the end of line 12 has been missed out.

Does the writer use words well and spell them correctly?

The writer misuses words. For example:

Line 2	*shopper*	should be	*shopping*
Line 7	*could*	should be	*got*

The writing has spelling mistakes. For example:

Line 1	*tipycal*	should be	*typical*
Line 11	*que*	should be	*queue*
Line 11	*supplys*	should be	*supplies*
Line 14	*vegatables*	should be	*vegetables*

Some words which can be troublesome are spelled correctly, however. For example: *automatically* (line 5), *trolley* (line 5), *wriggle* (line 10), *cupboards* (line 16).

What grade would you give this piece of writing?
On balance this is probably at the bottom of grade E. It is clumsy and inaccurate and the content is simple and unambitious.

Answer E

Does it describe the place well?
There is a lot of convincing detail here and a good sense of place and atmosphere. The writer is drawing on personal experience and has plenty to say. The observation is quite sharp. At times the writing is not as clear and direct as it might be, but it does share a common experience with the reader.

The content of this piece of writing is not a problem. Indeed there are some examples of experiences which cause a smile. The frustrations of the queue at the checkout is one of these.

Is it well organised?
The organisation is straightforward and obvious but completely logical. It follows the sequence of events from arrival to departure and does so in a sensible, controlled way. There is nothing wrong with a simple structure, if it is appropriate and it works.

Are the sentences clear and is the grammar correct?
The sentences are basically clear in content, and the writer does attempt to use quite complex sentences. However, there are many basic errors in sentence construction.

The first paragraph is a good beginning in many ways but the sentence construction of *The supermarket car park is full you drive down...* (line 1) is incorrect. In line 12, a conjunction such as 'and' or 'where' is necessary after *continue to the meat counter*. Line 16 onwards loses control of sentence construction and grammar, resulting in very clumsy writing.

Are the sentences properly punctuated?
The punctuation is rather thin and the mistakes are usually linked to mistakes in sentence construction. The writing has rather a rambling style, and would read more easily with a better use of commas and full stops.

Does the writer use words well and spell them correctly?
The writer does use words correctly, but there are some careless errors in spelling. For example:

Line 2	*untill*	should be	*until*
Line 6	*trollies*	should be	*trolleys*
Line 8	*brused*	should be	*bruised*
Line 9	*isle*	should be	*aisle*
Line 11	*tommorrow*	should be	*tomorrow*
Line 17	*akward*	should be	*awkward*

What grade would you give this piece of writing?
There is potential here and the writing has qualities of observation and ambition. However, the clumsiness in expression which results in a lack of direct and clear writing undermines the lively content. This might incline an examiner to grade it

at D rather than C. That said, it would not be too difficult to make it into a rather good piece of writing, resulting in a grade C. *Always* check your work for careless mistakes or slapdash expressions. Improving these areas could make the difference between being awarded a lower or higher grade.

2 Organizing your writing

page 16

Question 3

Most of the questions give advice on the *form* of the answer and *how to tackle it*:

	Form	How to tackle it
1	one-page handout	to make ten-year-old children aware...
2	letter	setting out ways ... could improve
3	—	set of topics to comment on
4	set of rules	'say why you have chosen them'
5	dialogue (conversation)	—
6	conversation	set the scene and make viewpoints clear
7	a lively article	suggested title and advice on approach

page 17

	Audience	Purpose
1	ten-year-old children	inform, explain
2	Environmental Department of the local council	explain, express opinion
3	not stated - the examiner	express opinion
4	your class	set out rules, express opinion
5	not stated - the examiner	express opinion
6	not stated - the examiner	express opinion
7	members of your school (and parents)	explain, express opinion

page 20

Our suggested order, starting with least formal, is:

6 The two people know each other well and would be relaxed - even if they didn't agree!

1 When writing for people younger than you, you should aim for an easy, relaxed style.

5 This would be more formal than question 6, but it is speech and so would be less formal than question 4.

4 If rules are written and to be followed by other people, they need to be fairly formal.

3 This one is tricky because the question doesn't make clear the kind of writing expected. It could be written quite informally and so come earlier in the order.
7 This magazine will be read by a range of different people so, although it should be friendly in tone, it shouldn't be too informal.
2 This is clearly the most formal situation – these are people you have almost certainly never met and you don't know what they will do with your letter – they might even read it out in a council meeting! So play safe.

page 27

Examiner's comments on Answer A

1 Tone
It is good that the candidate is addressing the reader directly but the tone could be a lot more positive. It is probably true that: 'the exams are getting near, and you had better be thinking.' The trouble is that this sounds more like a threat than something to stimulate the right kind of thinking about what to do next.

2 Remember your audience
The readers of a school magazine need help and support about what might happen after their examinations. In this article, you get a university degree 'if you're a swot' (line 7) not because you have worked hard and succeeded. A job is seen not as a positive choice but as the result of failing examinations. The article has been headed 'Life after school' but a reader might end up thinking it should be called 'Not much life after school'!

3 Get the facts right
There is an information problem here. The candidate has got it wrong about qualifications. If you fail at 16+, colleges provide courses to let you catch up (and so do many schools). You do not have to go out and get a job. There are also inaccuracies in what the candidate writes about college and university. When you use facts, you need to get them right.

4 Get the little things right
There are all sorts of little improvements that could be made to punctuation, vocabulary and sentence length. Some people cannot be bothered with the little details because they are only worth a few marks. It helps to remember that there is always someone on the borderline of pass/fail for a grade. That person only needs an extra mark. That person might be you.

Examiner's comments on Answer B

This is not a perfect article but it does all that could be expected for a high grade pass at 16+. Here are four things it does well.

1. It concentrates on a key point about life at 16+ – the way you should make your choice.
2. It sets out to be straightforward and supportive – and it is.
3. There is a good mixture of realism and encouragement to help its readers.
4. There is a mixture of shorter and longer sentences which makes the writing more varied.

3 Sentences and paragraphs

page 33

1 Question
2 Statement
3 Directive
4 Question
5 Exclamation

page 35

1 It
2 Everybody else in the family
3 Sarah
4 she
5 the cereal packet
6 The bread bin
7 There

page 37

1 is
2 should be
3 should unwrap
4 should be being driven
5 were depressed
6 should have thought
7 have … been

page 39

1 Maria *is* very keen on music.
2 She *started to learn* the piano five years ago.
3 Now she *has reached* Grade 5.
4 She *ought to be able to pass* it easily.
5 She *hopes to continue* her studies at the 6th Form College.
6 When we finally *reached* the top of Snowdon it *was snowing*.
7 So we *were unable to see* the route by which we *had ascended*.
8 It *would* soon *be getting* dark, and we *were* anxious about getting back safely.
9 Fortunately just as things *were looking* serious, the weather *began to break* and we *were able to follow* the railway track back down the mountain.

page 41

1 were
2 was
3 is
4 have
5 were

page 43

Verbs
he said - he'd given - said - had thrown - has thrown - had been working - appreciated

Ringed words
'now' should be 'then' in each case.

page 45

1 correct
2 They race for the fresh bread just coming out of the ovens.
3 Trolleys whizz up and down the aisles.
4 Children are crying (or 'cry') for a sweetie.
5 correct
6 correct

page 47

1 multiple
2 multiple
3 simple
4 multiple
5 multiple
6 simple
7 simple

page 48

1 Sentence **(a)** just tells us two facts. Sentence **(b)** suggests that the speaker is surprised at Eddie's result, considering he didn't do much work.
2 Sentence **(a)** tells us the speaker is going to do two things, but not the order in which they will be done. Sentence **(c)** tells us the order in which they will be done (swimming first, visit afterwards). Sentence **(b)** tells us that the speaker will do one of two things.
3 In these three sentences the people did the same two things. Sentence **(c)** just gives us the information. Sentence **(b)** also tells us which came first. Sentence **(a)** suggests that walking home was an unusual thing to do.
4 Sentence **(c)** just tells us the facts. Sentence **(a)** suggests that being able to drive a car at sixteen is unusual. Sentence **(b)** looks like part of an argument. The speaker is suggesting that people of sixteen can't normally drive, so either she's sixteen or she can drive, but - by implication - both statements cannot be true.

page 51

One version could be:

The crowd went wild, shouting, 'Michael, Michael, Michael!', so he came on again to do a couple more songs. Usually in the song, 'She's out of my life', he collapses, but he didn't collapse: he threw himself onto the stage. Everyone screamed in excitement, but when he stood up, his nose was all mashed up all over his face.

page 56

This is how the original article was divided into paragraphs. (They are numbered for convenience.)

1 In the early 1950s, Walt Disney conceived a theme park where his already hugely popular cartoon characters - Micky Mouse, Donald Duck and the rest - could come to life, to enchant children and make their Uncle Walt even richer. Anaheim was chosen as the location for Disneyland on the basis that these acres of orange groves, thirty miles southeast of downtown, would become LA's next focus of population growth - which indeed they did. The whole area is now overrun with hotels and restaurants (when Disney opened his next theme park, in Florida, he made sure he owned all of them too, thus retaining total corporate control), and the boom doesn't look like slowing. If you're not coming to see Disneyland, you may as well give the place a miss: it hasn't an ounce of interest in itself.

2 To make the most of Disneyland - the ultimate escapist fantasy and the blueprint for imitations worldwide - throw yourself right into it. Don't think twice about anything and go on every ride you can. The high admission price (£25) includes them all, although during peak periods each one can entail hours of queueing. Remember, too, that the emphasis is on family fun; the authorities take a dim view of anything remotely anti-social and eject those that they consider guilty.

3 Over four hundred 'imaginers' worked to create the Indiana Jones Adventure, Disneyland's biggest opening in years. Two hours of queueing are built into the ride, with an interactive archaeological dig and 1930s-style newsreel show leading up to the main feature – a giddy journey along 2500ft of skull-encrusted corridors in which you face fireballs, falling rubble, venomous snakes and, inevitably, a rolling boulder finale.

4 Among the best of the older rides are two in Adventureland: the Pirates of the Caribbean, a boat trip through underground caverns, singing along with drunken pirates; and the Haunted Mansion, a riotous 'doom buggy' tour in the company of the house spooks. Tomorrowland is Disney's vision of the future, where the Space Mountain roller-coaster zips through the pitch-blackness of outer space, and Michael Jackson dances in 3-D. The Skyway cable cars that connect it with the clever but cloyingly sentimental Fantasyland are the only spot in the park from which you can see the outside world.

5 As for accommodation, try to visit Disneyland just for the day and spend the night somewhere else. Most of the hotels and motels nearby cost well in excess of £50 per night. You're not permitted to bring your own food to the park; you can only consume fast food produced on the premises. Disneyland is at 1313 Harbor Blvd, Anaheim, 45 minutes by car from downtown using the Santa Ana Freeway. In summer, the park is open daily between 8am and 1am; otherwise opening hours are weekdays 10am to 6pm, Saturday 9am to midnight, and Sunday 9am to 10pm.

Paragraph topics

1 Lead paragraph, setting the scene and providing background information.

2 Outlines how visitors can make the most of Disneyland, and some of the drawbacks.

3 Focuses on the good and bad points of one of the rides.

4 Describes two further rides considered to be 'among the best'.

5 Conclusion and factual details.

4 Punctuation

page 63

1 The student who needs to improve their use of:
  (**a**) full stops is C
  (**b**) question marks is A
  (**c**) exclamation marks is B.

Correct versions:

A The lottery makes life enjoyable, what is wrong with that?

B It gives people the chance to dream about being multi-millionaires. As for the prize money being too large, get serious! Who wouldn't be happy if they won so much? I would.

C I am writing to you because of what the reverend said. I think that what he said is rubbish because if you win the lottery jackpot you don't have to work ever again. Your children won't have to work and if your family need help, or friends, (financially wise) you can sort it out for them.

page 65

1 Words in which capital letters are wrongly used:

AlwayS, *Family*, *She*, *Just*, *Owned*, *Side*, *Scientist*, *Who*, *Special*, *Safe*, *Suit*, *Probably*, *Most*, *OF*.

The words which the writer forgot to give a capital letter:

On, *He*.

2 **(a)** In the distance I could see that Darren had already started the Ford Fiesta and was pulling away from the Southgate test centre.

(b) Suddenly I realised there was a problem: Mr Steep, his instructor, had already got out of the car, but the examiner, Mr Acton, had not yet got in. Realising what had happened, Mother began to run after the car as Darren gathered speed and turned the corner into Bell Street.

(c) Both Darren, Mother and the Fiesta disappeared from view. There was a sudden squeal of brakes, a scream of, 'No!' from my mother and a loud crash.

(d) This would make a good entry for the book 'How to Fail Your Driving Test' by Ivor Smash, I decided.

(e) Since Darren had run over a fox and hit a lamp post, we had to call out both the R.S.P.C.A. and the A.A. When Dad and I asked him about it, all Darren could say was, 'Perhaps I need a new pair of glasses.'

page 67

1 **(a)** Boxer became faithful to the pigs because he could not think things out for himself, so he accepted the pigs as his teachers and believed everything that was told to him.

(b) Well it's up to you to make your choice but always do your best and you will succeed.

(c) I'm writing to you in concern about an article I read in a magazine.

2 **(a)** An individual shouted, 'The King is back from the dead.'

(b) The two films are based on the same thing, nuclear war, but they are very different. 'When the Wind Blows' is a cartoon and 'Threads' is a drama documentary.

(c) The supermarket aisle was filled with potatoes, fresh carrots and cauliflowers and a wonderfully earthy smell, I would have preferred the … meat section. Here the carnivores were readily buying the half price beef that was on offer.

3 'First off, I'm a chef, not a cook. I get wound up by that mistake. I don't like the word 'cook' – I'm more of an artiste than that.

I left school after doing work experience here one summer, and I've been an apprentice for eight months. Hopefully, I'll end up as a celebrity chef with my own restaurant like Marco Pierre-White.

Nobody's ever called me a girl. In fact people are quite impressed because my job's unusual.'

page 69

1 **(a)** He said they treated him like dirt. He said, 'I can get a job easily, I can be a barman.' I laughed and went home.
(A comma is needed before opening a piece of direct speech which is mid-sentence.)

(b) The Editor,
Daily Mail,
London.
(If you are going to use commas in an address they have to be used all the way through, except at the end when you need a full stop.)

(c) While packing up, Julia found her long lost silver ring.
(A comma is needed so that Julia does not sound like she is being packed too!)

2 **(a)** American football, which is played on a pitch marked with parallel lines, is sometimes known as 'gridiron football'.

(b) Similar to the game of rugby, American football is a contact sport.

(c) An oval ball and rugby-like goal posts are used but, unlike rugby, players have to be well-padded and wear helmets.

(d) Only eleven players, although there are many more in a team, are allowed on the pitch at any one time.

(e) A game has four quarters, and a quarter lasts fifteen minutes.

3 **(a)** Though Andy kept on watching, the football tackles alarmed him.

(b) The referee blew his whistle at Paul, and his team mates began to jeer.

(c) The policewoman, who was carrying Cantona's shoe, jumped onto the horse.

(d) The bill had to be paid but the team's manager had disappeared.

(e) Since there was no one else around, the goalkeeper tried on the thin captain's suit.

page 71

1 **(a)** Contestants win one of these prizes: a holiday, a television, a car or a cuddly toy.

(b) The rules in this game are simple: the first one to answer wins the point.

2 The students could have improved their coursework like this:

(a) And finally the shop manager: a breed that evolved through managing to do as little work as possible and looking extremely similar to a Butlin's red coat.

(b) A few days after I moved in we were brought together and introduced as: 'Annie, your friend' and 'Jo, your new friend' respectively.

3 **i** + **(c)** When his luck ran out and he had gambled his last penny, he played

the guitar and begged; when things went better and he won, he would stay in a room at the Ritz.

ii + (d) The Minister said that the parents must sign the contracts too; if any of them refused, then it would only make the situation worse.

iii + (e) The holiday brochure promised a mesmerising view from the roof garden; two pots of peonies and a glimpse of the local bus station weren't quite what she had expected.

iv + (a) The cost of rugby shirts has increased once again; perhaps a sponsor can be persuaded to donate some extra funds.

v + (b) It was getting late: the wedding guests had got lost; if only they had been given a map, rather than being told to follow James.

page 73

1 **(a)** But he clearly loves dogs - that, or he has them for protection.

(b) As you are crossing keep looking and don't run - you could fall over. But don't walk slower than a snail - you will want to get across the road before the next car comes speeding along.

or

As you are crossing keep looking and don't run (you could fall over). But don't walk slower than a snail - you will want to get across the road before the next car comes speeding along.

2 **(a)** Marie - who hated all reptiles - was longing to go back to the hotel.

(b) 'For years tourists were not allowed to visit turtle beaches after dark - their torches might mislead the turtles,' explained the guide.

(c) Hearing a turtle lumbering towards her, Marie switched on her light - it wasn't every day she had the chance to confuse a tortoise.

(d) The turtles were plodding a long way up the beaches - they needed to lay their eggs above the high tide mark.

(e) Some day the baby turtles would hatch - no doubt looking like miniature prehistoric monsters.

3 Having problems finding some get-up-and-go in the mornings? New 'Lemon and Mint' shampoo and conditioner for oily hair from Original Mint Source have the most invigorating fragrance we've ever tried - guaranteed to wake up the laziest of sleepyheads.

page 74

1 + 2 The article was showing the plight of the Indians living in the Amazon. I was deeply shocked by the information it gave and feel as though I should do something to help.

3 + 4 The Indians are being pursued by Brazilian timber cutters to let them cut down the rain forest for the mahogany trade. These forests are the Indian's lifeline and taking it away means death for the Indians.

5 + 6 If the Indians refuse, after seeing through the deception and greed of the 'timber cutters' who by now will have tried everything from bribery to threatening behaviour, then their lives become under threat from these dangerous people. There are accounts of these 'timber cutters' opening fire on tribes of helpless Indians, killing women and children too.

(You could argue that **3** + **4** + **5** + **6** should form one paragraph.)

page 75

This is how the original article was divided into paragraphs:

Quail eggs seemed the ideal exotic starter for Ann Brewer's dinner party.

Three weeks later, she gave her friends even more to talk about by hatching chicks from three of them.

Mrs Brewer took the eggs off the menu after accidentally breaking one and finding it to be fertile. So she put the remaining 11 in an incubator and chose melon as a substitute first course.

Now she has hatched eight more quail chicks after buying a further two dozen brown speckled eggs from her local branch of Waitrose.

Mrs Brewer, a 59-year-old poultry breeder, explained: 'It was a case of placing them under a lamp in the warm and waiting to see what happened.

'As long as the eggs are fertile and the yolks haven't been broken then they should hatch.'

Mrs Brewer, who also runs kennels with her husband William near Petersfield, Hampshire, said the 11 young birds would be sold to a breeder.

Fertilised quail eggs have a small white spot in the yolk. In Britain, quail – a small game bird the size of a pigeon – is regarded as a delicacy. An estimated nine million of its eggs are eaten each year, selling for £1.20 per dozen.

Mrs Brewer's eggs were supplied by the FayreGame company. Managing director Nick White said hens were put in to lay at six weeks – an age when it is difficult to identify and exclude male birds.

He added: 'I would say that five per cent of quail eggs on the shelves are fertile. They are absolutely harmless.'

page 76

1 SPECIAL OFFER: 3rd night free Nov. 1 – Dec. 24 '96 & '97 and Jan. 2 – Mar. 20 & Jul./Aug.

2 LONDON & SOUTH EAST: There will be some sunny spells but also showers, heavy at times. Max. 8C. (46F.)

page 78

1 **(a)** 'What is the matter?' Jenny's mum said.
'It's not fair, they keep picking on me!' Jenny cried.
'Why, what have they done?' replied Mum sympathetically.

(b) 'No, I'd better not because I'm having my dinner soon,' said Jeremy.
'Okay then, we'll see you at school on Monday,' said Colin. 'Bye,' they all shouted.

2 **(a)** The examiner asked, 'Can you explain how factory farming works?'

(b) 'Poultry or animals are housed in confined spaces,' Tara said.

(c) Then, pointing at the photograph, she continued, 'They're fed on high protein foods.'

(d) 'Yes,' said the examiner, 'and do you know anything else about the feed stuffs?'

(e) 'No,' Tara admitted, 'but I know that battery hens lay more eggs than free range chickens.'

page 80

1 (a) INTERVIEWER: Hello this is Radio 1! Now I'm going to be speaking to a professional arcade machine gambler, who claims to be earning £120 a day from machines.

TERRY: Yes, that's right, well, on average.

The names of characters should be in capital letters. The speeches should not be enclosed in quotation marks.

(b) INTER.: Hello, Mr Freeman.

MR FREE.: Hello, how are you?

The names of characters should be in capital letters. A colon is needed after the name of the character.

2 This is our version of the speeches:

KAREN: The concert tickets cost fifty pounds.
MARK: I don't have the money on me.
KAREN: Can you give me the money the next time you see me?
MARK: I'll have to borrow some money from my mother.
KAREN: Will your mother lend you the money?
MARK: I'm not sure, but she might.
KAREN: How are you going to pay your mother back?
MARK: I'll be starting a Saturday job working in a computer shop next month.
KAREN: It's great news that you have got a job!
MARK: Have you had any luck looking for work?
KAREN: I baby-sit regularly for Jo, my neighbour, but I don't want a Saturday job because I need to have that time free to get my schoolwork done.

page 81

Different choices are possible. However, by reading the reasons given for the answers below, you will at least gain some ideas of how to work out which punctuation marks to use.

1 A hand written note, scribbled in green ink, was taped firmly across the letter box.
This is neither formal or informal so commas are suitable.

2 The tour of the docks (built in 1905) will begin at 2.30 p.m.
This seems more formal, so use brackets.

3 Readers of the 'Daily Herald' will be pleased to know that Lui Chan, who once played for Torton Wanderers, has offered to coach the team.
A report which is written in a relaxed style is not too formal so commas are suitable.

4 'Well, it was like this: the lads who had come on the trip - some of them as young as thirteen - had just got a bit bored with waiting ...'
This is written in a chatty style and the underlined phrase comes within speech, so choosing dashes would be fine.

5 The court should know that Michael Smith (the defendant) has up until now always been thought of as one of Lightwater High School's best students.
This is a formal report, so use brackets.

6 Thank you for the beautiful coat. It was just right - green has always been my favourite colour - and I shall really enjoy wearing it this winter.
This is an informal letter so choosing dashes would be fine.

page 82

Capital letters

1 Donna had just filled the front of her trolley from the fruit and vegetable section at Tesco's when she remembered the magazine for her mother.

2 Leaving the trolley by the bananas she went to collect 'Art of Good Cooking' before continuing with her shopping.

3 Up and down the aisles she steered, remembering the Shredded Wheat, Coca Cola, bread, rice, custard powder, and even that they preferred Brazilian coffee beans.

4 In the household goods aisle, she noticed a stranger staring into her trolley. Donna headed away from the cans of Mr Sheen polish and towards the check-out.

5 One last treat. She would have a chocolate bar. Placing the Crunchie on the conveyor belt Donna began to pile up her shopping behind it.

6 'These aren't mine,' she said holding up a punnet of strawberries, 'nor these!' She had found a bag of pears.

7 'No,' came a voice from behind her, 'they're mine.'
It was the stranger who had stared at her trolley.

8 'Someone took my trolley from beside the bananas,' he said. 'It must have been you.'

Full stops

1 Tom knew this was the dog he wanted when the Alsatian chewed at his trainers.

2 'Are you sure?' Sandy was not pleased, 'I don't want our home destroyed!'

3 Well he ... er ... he's probably just hungry. I'm sure that, once he's fed regularly, he'll stop.'

4 'You should ask the R.S.P.C.A. officer whether this dog will be happy in a small flat.'

page 83

Apostrophe

1 'There's no way I'll be home by ten,' said Chris.
2 Both the tyres on Chris's bike were completely flat.
3 'They've been cut – there's a hole in each of 'em,' Chris said.
4 'Don't worry. You'd better borrow mine. It's over there,' Alex offered.
5 'No, it's not,' Chris said. 'Its saddle is, but the rest of it's gone.'

Quotation marks

1 'Do you keep back copies of "The Times"?' she asked the librarian.
2 'No,' he said, 'but we do have CD-Roms of "The Times" and "The Guardian".'
3 'Good, I'm looking for an article about an episode of "Panorama". I think it was called "Watching the Detectives",' she explained.
4 'I remember that,' he said, 'wasn't it about video camera surveillance?'

page 84

General test A

I only paid £3 for Hermie, my pet hamster, but he's ended up costing almost £1000.

It all started one Friday evening at our hotel-pub in the Isle of Man. I'd just taken Hermie out of his cage when my dog Sue, a bull mastiff, ran into my bedroom and knocked us both flying.

Hermie was so scared, he hid in a tiny hole in the skirting and wouldn't budge. I tried to put my hand in to get him out, but the hole was too small.

Dad said Hermie would come out when he was ready, but I was worried he'd starve to death, so I persuaded Dad to remove the floorboards. He and my uncle couldn't remove them completely, 'cause of my fitted wardrobes, but they wedged a few open.

There was no sign of Hermie in the morning, and after we'd waited all afternoon to no avail, Dad started nailing down the floorboards.

Suddenly, Dad accidentally hit a hot-water-pipe! By the time a plumber arrived, my bed was soaking and water was seeping into the pub below. Then the plumber scratched my wardrobes ripping up the boards. I thought Dad would flip when he had to replaster the bar ceiling, but he was really understanding.

Then, on Sunday evening, Dad heard a scratching from behind a wall. He was sure it was Hermie, but there was a radiator in the way. Dad didn't want to raise my hopes, so while I was at school, he secretly arranged to rescue him.

He cut a huge hole above the radiator, but when he looked in Hermie was too far to reach. Then mum squeezed his water bottle down the gap and when he crawled up to have a drink, she grabbed him.

He was skinny and dirty and his little paws were bleeding, but at least he was alive. The repair bill came to around £1000. And we thought hamsters were cheap pets!

page 85

General test B

A young inner-city family from London stayed with us the other day and it is clear that, in the past year or so, the designer fashion craze has become an epidemic.

Not only do the young, and even the very young, demand the latest in designer wear – Calvin Klein, Ralph Lauren, Armani, Timberland, Versace, Moschino, Carhart, Tommy Hilfiger and so on – they hardly now dare venture on the street unless they have it. They were once judged by the brand name on their trainers; they are now judged according to the label attached to their polo shirts, designer jeans and jackets.

And copies, which abound, are spotted immediately. They may be almost identical to the real thing, but they don't bear the all-important serial number. Only the genuine best is acceptable if you are to have any street-credibility. Even the sunglasses have to come from Asprey's.

Our friend, the young mother, who had three children, displayed genuine alarm – fear even – at the extent of the problem.

She said: 'You look at the kids hanging about a tenement block in a very poor area – some of them as young as 10 – and you have to ask yourself: "How can they afford those clothes?" Some of them are wearing £400 or £500 worth. The answer is they can't afford it. They have to steal for what they are wearing – or parents have to. Even the babies wear Chipie designer stuff worth £200.'

The truth is that whereas the outside world links young crime in the inner cities with drugs, it is as often as not associated with the sort of clothes seen in Bond Street. Says our friend, 'Often the kids have the stuff torn off them and are left naked. It's terrifying.'

Would making pupils wear a strictly enforced school uniform take some of the pressure off parents and children? Might it reduce the number of youth crimes? What do you think?

page 86

General test C

Silent rail passengers who never complain about delays, ask the way to the buffet, or try to strike up conversation are to make an appearance on a seaside branch line.

The 'passengers', life-sized papier maché dummies, are to be placed on trains between Hull and Bridlington as part of a community arts project. Others will stand or sit at station platforms.

The dummies will ride on the trains from the end of next month. Some will be dressed in period costumes of the Yorkshire working families who came to Bridlington for their holidays earlier this century.

They will be made in a disused parcel office at Bridlington station. Passengers, tourists and local people will be encouraged to help construct them.

Shirley Hester of the mental health charity MIND, which is involved with the project, said: 'We hope that people living all along the line will come to help us with the sculptures and even people on holiday for a few days who would like to try their hand at making an arm or a foot. We hope it will liven up the station and add to the interest of the journey.'

Ken Bray, a spokesman for Regional Railways North East, said: 'The models will always be accompanied by one or two fare-paying adults.'

5 Words and spelling

page 91

curtilage: a yard or small piece of land attached to a house
cogue: a wooden pail
bocasin: soft cotton cloth
quern: a hand mill for grinding grain
mandola: a stringed musical instrument, forerunner of the mandolin

page 93

These are to some extent a matter of opinion, but we suggest:
(a) weak - ineffectual - feeble
(b) pushover - switched off - dud
(c) wimp - wet - nerd

page 94

tear+ful	un+expected+ly	regret(t)+able	fortunate+ly
hyper+market	pro+life	dis+agree+ment	over+weight+y
un+clean+able	en+large+ment		

page 95

These are not the only possibilities. If in doubt about other words, check in a dictionary.

hooded	swiftly	miner
delightful	headless, header, heading, headship	simplify, simply
foolish	excitable, excitement	birdlike
sightless, sighted	referee	regretful, regrettable

page 97

hyperactive: more than normally active, unhealthily so
megaphone: a loud-hailer
ultrasonic: above the frequency of audible sound

autosuggestion: making yourself believe something, or feel something without realising you are doing it
circumnavigate: sail around (something)
contra-indication: something that suggests or proves the opposite opinion

page 98

1	2	3
clean	enlarge	examinability
cleanable	enlarged	examinable
cleaned	enlargement	examinant
cleaner	enlarger	examinate
cleaning	largeness	examination
cleanish	re-enlarge	examinative
cleanlily	unenlarged	examinator
cleanliness	unlarge	examinatorial
cleanly		examinatory
cleanness		examine
self-cleaning		examinee
self-cleansing		examiner
unclean		examining
uncleanable		pre-examination
uncleaned		pre-examine
uncleanliness		re-examinable
uncleanly		re-examinate
		re-examination
		re-examine
		self-examination
		unexaminable
		unexamined
		unexamining

page 100

Line	Wrong spelling	Correct spelling
1	catridge	cartridge
4	to	two
6	litrature	literature
8	litrature	literature
10	excitidly	excitedly
14	likly	likely
14	worring	worrying
16	excitidly	excitedly
17	diffrence	difference
19	propper	proper
25	excepts	accepts

page 104

pianos	bushes	halves	babies
keys	wrinkles	shoes	taxes
taxis	heroes	cutlasses	roofs

page 105

word	+ing	+ed
repel	repelling	repelled
queue	queueing	queued
try	trying	tried
tape	taping	taped
reveal	revealing	revealed
tip	tipping	tipped
pay	paying	paid
defer	deferring	deferred
happen	happening	happened
sharpen	sharpening	sharpened
peel	peeling	peeled
budget	budgeting	budgeted

page 106

1 hopefully, shyly, recently, dully, fortunately, dottily, beautifully, surely
2 quicker, quickest, smaller, smallest, drier, driest, madder, maddest, saner, sanest, crueller, cruellest

page 112

accelerate
accommodation
address
assist
beginning
brilliant
caterpillar
collapse
correct
commit
corridor
disappear
embarrass
exaggerate
gorilla
harass
imitate
mattress
millennium
necessary
occasion
omit
parallel
pedal
possess
professional
sheriff
sufficient
terrible
unnecessary
woollen

page 113

1 except
2 There
3 whether
4 past
5 lie
6 knew/have
7 lose
8 all together
9 affect
10 Who's
11 canvas
12 licence
13 bail *or* bale
14 site
15 council
16 calendar
17 where/stationary
18 metres
19 lead/needed/lightening
20 kerb

6 Common errors

page 116

1 advise
2 among
3 accept
4 effect
5 illusion

page 120

1 Correct
2 Wrong – it should be *colander*
3 Wrong – you can only use *both* when there are two; here there are three. *Both* should be left out
4 Correct
5 Wrong – it should be council

page 124

1 Wrong – it should be '... up to my mother and *me* ...'
2 Wrong – it should be *fewer*
3 Correct
4 Wrong – it should be *metres*
5 Correct

page 127

1 *red* (should be *read*)
past (should be *passed*)
2 *Practise* (should be *Practice*)
To (should be *Two*)
3 *wether* (should be *weather*)
wether (should be *whether*)
4 Correct
5 *through* (should be *threw*)
who's (should be *whose*)